Bullock Cart to Business

'I remember Debendra as one of my favourite Master's Students at IIT Kharagpur. We are similar in many respects. We both belong to the tribal dominated district of Mayurbhanj. We both had very humble beginnings. We both did our graduation from NIT Rourkela. Bullock carts were our primary modes of transport. For my schooling, I used to travel overnight, go across two rivers, by bullock cart from my village to the hostel. During vacations, I used to help my parents with their agriculture. Bullocks were an integral part of our family; they help us with ploughing as well as harvesting of the crop. While Debendra entered the corporate world and established his company in Japan, I pursued a career as a teacher.

'His journey from a remote village in India to the corporate world of Japan is truly inspiring. *Bullock Cart to Business* is an excellent read for those who may want to follow in his footsteps.'

—**Professor Damodar Acharya**
Former Director, IIT Kharagpur

'I visited India for the first time after meeting Debendra. The country's energy in terms of its people, goods and infrastructure left a lasting impression on me.

'I always feel that a business should connect people from different countries with different cultures, and I am convinced that Deb's business acts as a bridge between India and Japan.

'I deeply respect his friendly personality, understanding of both cultures and determination. After reading his life story in *Bullock Cart to Business*, I know for a fact that no one else could have established synergy between Japan and Odisha.'

—**Mitsuhiro Iwanaga**
President, Arrows Opthalmic

'I have known Debendra Mohanta for 20 years and have been impressed by the way he values people over business profit. He combines his expertise and sensitivity to benefit those around him. *Bullock Cart to Business* integrates his knowledge and philosophy, along with his experience, offering valuable insights for those looking to succeed in various countries. His approach emphasizes the importance of human relationships and communication, with his success rooted in building trust and growing together. The book provides practical advice, which can be beneficial for business expansion in different cultures and markets.'

—**Kei Yamaguchi**
Director, IT Alcon

'I know Debendra as a leading IT personnel for global system implementation and rollouts. His knowledge of business and IT, merged with the Japanese way of doing things, has really helped us with some critical projects in the past. He regularly meets with me, even though I'm retired now, to share his enthusiasm and ideas about his entrepreneurship journey.

'I am happy that he has shared his story in *Bullock Cart to Business*, which will benefit and inspire many young minds to know what it takes to succeed.'

—**Yoshisada Takahashi**
Former CIO and President,
Information Strategy Division, Komatsu Ltd.

Bullock Cart to Business

Memoirs of an Odisha Boy

DEBENDRA MOHANTA

Published by
Rupa Publications India Pvt. Ltd 2025
7/16, Ansari Road, Daryaganj
New Delhi 110002

Sales centres:
Bengaluru Chennai
Hyderabad Jaipur Kathmandu
Kolkata Mumbai Prayagraj

Copyright © Debendra Mohanta 2025

The views and opinions expressed in this book are the author's own and the facts are as reported by him, which have been verified to the extent possible, and the publishers are not in any way liable for the same.

The publisher has used its best endeavours to ensure that URLs for external websites referred to in this book are correct and active at the time of going to press. However, the publisher has no responsibility for the websites and can make no guarantee that a site will remain live or that the content is or will remain appropriate.

All rights reserved.
No part of this publication may be reproduced, transmitted or stored in a retrieval system, in any form or by any means, electronic, mechanical, photocopying, recording or otherwise, without the prior permission of the publisher.

P-ISBN: 978-93-6156-695-0
E-ISBN: 978-93-6156-906-7

First impression 2025

10 9 8 7 6 5 4 3 2 1

The moral right of the author has been asserted.

Printed in India

This book is sold subject to the condition that it shall not, by way of trade or otherwise, be lent, resold, hired out or otherwise circulated, without the publisher's prior consent, in any form of binding or cover other than that in which it is published.

To
my parents
the late Sitanath Mohanta
and
the late Kesabati Mohanta

Contents

Foreword	ix
Introduction	xi
1. Jashipur and Beyond	1
2. Engineering My Dream	13
3. When Work Is Fun	24
4. Leading from the Front	34
5. Onwards and Upwards!	43
6. Looking East	50
7. Expansion and Consolidation	61
8. The Calamity and After	75
9. Moving Ahead and Moving On	85
10. Settling Down at L&T	93
11. Business Takes Off	101
12. Consolidation and the COVID-19 Challenge	111
13. Steering Towards a New Direction	121
14. Focus on Odisha	127
15. Japan–India and Mayurbhanj	137
16. Unlocking Odisha's Potential	150
17. Meeting Inspirational Leaders	170
Acknowledgements	177

Foreword

The story of resurgent Odisha is one that deserves to be talked about, more so because the state was at the bottom in nearly every development indicator. Today, it is high up in the list of states that have attracted maximum domestic investments. All-round progress has touched the lives of the state's residents from all segments and strata of society.

I am glad that Debendra Mohanta has, in his memoir, highlighted Odisha's recent successes as well as the challenges that lie ahead. As a son of Odisha, he has done well for himself, establishing his credentials in far-off Japan—first as a corporate executive with stints at various reputed Indian IT companies and then more recently as an independent entrepreneur. This book is an account of his early life in his home town of Jashipur in Mayurbhanj, the challenges he faced while pursuing higher studies, his move to Japan and his successful journey thereafter.

What pleases me the most is that throughout his career and stay in Japan, Debendra never lost touch with his home state. More heartening is that he has launched various initiatives, working closely with educational institutions and the administration of Odisha, to empower the youth by providing avenues in training and skill development to make them employment-worthy. He has gone a step further by assisting them with job placements.

Debendra's story, which he tells honestly and with a sense of modest simplicity, should be an inspiration to millions of people not just in Odisha but across the country. I am sure that thousands of youths in Odisha could make it big, but they have to go the extra mile, just as Debendra did, to make it happen. More importantly, I hope that like Debendra, they will share their success with Odisha.

I wish Debendra Mohanta all the very best in his life and career and hope that his bond with Odisha and his commitment to the state's development will grow stronger in the future.

—**Mohan Charan Majhi**
Chief Minister, Odisha

Introduction

People who knew I was working on a book that narrated my personal and professional journey would often ask me how I got the idea to write it. After establishing myself in Japan first as a corporate executive and then as an independent entrepreneur, I visited India on several occasions for personal and professional reasons. During those trips, I was invited by universities and other institutions to deliver talks to share my life experiences with the youth, and I found enormous interest among the audience in what I had to say. I wondered if there was a more expansive way to reach a large audience.

Some of my friends suggested I pen those experiences in the form of a book that would tell my journey from the small town of Jashipur in Odisha to Tokyo in Japan. I later came into contact with a few people associated with the Kalinga Literary Festival (KLF) held annually in Bhubaneswar, who also encouraged me.

It was during the 2023 KLF that I met Sanjeev Sanyal—an author who, at the time of writing, was a full-time member of the Prime Minister's Economic Advisory Council—and was motivated by his talk. KLF founder and director Rashmi Ranjan Parida nudged me, though I was still reluctant then, to write. Incidentally, I also spoke at the festival and interacted with a Japanese literature professor in a panel discussion.

In addition to sharing my experiences with others, I had two main purposes for writing this book. The first was to encourage the youth of rural Odisha to have the courage to try out different career trajectories that may seem unreachable. Not just Odisha but most of India is still predominantly rural, and the people residing in the countryside have enormous potential to make it big in life. The second purpose was more personal. I wanted to lay out my own roadmap for the next few years. Through this book, I have been able to concretize those plans in my mind and the way ahead.

While pursuing my career in Japan, there was barely a year when I did not visit my home state of Odisha; sometimes, I made more than one trip a year, both for personal and professional reasons. When I relocated to Japan, I was worried about the conditions in Odisha in terms of both social indicators and business and infrastructure issues. Odisha was considered one of the underdeveloped states, even though it had a robust reserve of natural resources (minerals and metals). It had also gained worldwide infamy for starvation deaths. Nevertheless, I was hopeful of a turnaround—even if it took time—provided we had a government committed to the state's well-being and willing to bite the bullet when it came to formulating and implementing revolutionary policies and programmes. When Naveen Patnaik took over the reins of the government in 2000, things began to change, and with time, those changes developed momentum.

In this book, I have written about those changes. I do not say that everything is fine in my home state today; indeed, there is a lot more that needs to be done in areas of social upliftment, education, health and general infrastructure. For instance, in the Social Progress Index, Odisha falls in the 'low social progress' category.[1] However, it is also true that the Odisha of today is far more developed than it was two decades ago. We don't have starvation deaths; health services have reached all corners of the state; the educational set-up is more aligned to the needs of industry and focused on skill development, and infrastructure has improved. Former Chief Minister Naveen Patnaik was at the helm of these changes, and due to his commitment to the promises made, his party was repeatedly elected to power since he assumed charge. Although his party lost the recent assembly elections and he had to relinquish his post, he will be remembered as one of the few successful chief ministers India has had in recent decades.

The long road that Odisha has travelled in the last two decades is evident from the following facts: according to a study by a prominent trade body, in 2009, the state became the second-most attractive domestic investment destination.[2]

---

[1] Kapoor, Amit, and Michael Green, 'Social Progress Index: States and Districts of India', *Institute for Competitiveness and Government of India*, 2 January 2023, https://tinyurl.com/3xzfvbs3. Accessed on 20 December 2024.

[2] Patnaik, Nageshwar, 'Orissa Second to Gujarat in India Inc's Investment Plans in 2009', *The Economic Times*, 13 February 2010, https://tinyurl.com/42szbjps. Accessed on 18 February 2025.

1
Jashipur and Beyond

Today, Jashipur is a bustling town in Odisha's Mayurbhanj district, with good road connectivity to important cities in the state and many schools and colleges. It also has a court and a tehsildar's office. Bordering Jharkhand and West Bengal, it is roughly 300 km from Rourkela and only a little over 200 km from the capital city of Bhubaneswar and falls on the Vijayawada–Ranchi and Chennai–Kolkata national highways. Not too far away is the famous Similipal National Park, known for the Khairi tiger. Rairangpur, President Droupadi Murmu's native town, which also happens to be my in-laws' place, is nearby.

However, when I was born on 27 June 1971, Jashipur was a semi-rural block. There were no buses, and residents had to depend mainly on bullock carts and bicycles. Because the Similipal forest was nearby, several trucks plied the route, carrying timber to the sub-district of Karanjia and then to faraway places for further transportation. Jashipur residents would strike deals with the drivers for a lift to places along the way. There were only a few schools, all Odiya medium; Jashipur had no colleges, so those aspiring to study further had to move to distant places such as Cuttack and beyond.

These were some of Jashipur's many shortcomings, but none bothered me much as a child. I was happy to be with my family, who loved and cared for me. I had many avenues for passing the time with my friends, with whom I played *gilli-danda*, climbed trees to pluck mangoes (raw and ripe), took joyrides on bullock carts and did everything a child without a care in the world would do in a normal environment. Jashipur was my world.

My father, Sitanath Mohanta, had completed his minor, which meant that he had passed the seventh standard. It was a big achievement in those days, and he was offered a government job. He might have taken it up or even studied further, but my grandfather, Narahari Mohanta, persuaded him to take care of the family's considerable landholding. We owned nearly 60 acres of cultivable land, and although my grandfather gave away 20 acres to one of my aunts, we were still left with 40 acres, which was quite a lot. We cultivated various crops but primarily paddy. We also grew vegetables, sesame, etc.

My grandfather's decision came after he realized that his son, my uncle, was not interested in agriculture. Instead, he occupied himself with resolving disputes among people and working as a go-between involving the people and government offices, for which he received a commission. Seeing his lack of interest in farming, my grandfather divided the property. My uncle began living separately, while we stayed with my grandparents in the ancestral house, which was half mud and half brick and mortar.

My grandfather needed a helping hand, more so because he was visually impaired. The story of the loss of his eyesight is indeed tragic. When he was in his forties, he contracted conjunctivitis during the monsoon season. Troubled by the persistent eyesore, he asked a friend for advice. This friend was in the business of brewing country liquor, and he suggested that a few drops of his freshly made concoction would cure him. He assured my grandfather of the treatment's efficacy, which he claimed had been successfully tested on other patients. To this day, I don't understand how my grandfather believed such nonsense. The result was that those few drops robbed him of his eyesight forever. Being close to him, one of the things I loved doing was to take him to a nearby tea stall named Chattish Tea Shop for breakfast and tea and then to Saitu Pan Shop every morning. The fact that he could not see did not lessen his zest for life.

While my father could not continue his studies, he made sure that his five children, three daughters and two sons—I was the youngest—studied as much and for as long as they wanted. His children's names are Mahesh, Khaira, Parbati and Damyanti.

The eldest of my siblings, my brother Mahesh, was sixteen years older than me. I have no memory of my brother's and sisters' school days, except those of Damyanti, the youngest of my sisters. One reason for the recollection is that she was my mentor and guide during my early years in school. She was especially close to my parents and was everyone's darling.

When I was four years old, I would accompany her to the local school. I was not eligible to attend because only children over five could get admission to the first grade. So for a full year, I was an informal or unofficial student. Thus, my parents ensured that I was gainfully occupied instead of running around and creating mischief. When I properly joined the first grade at the same Jashipur Upper Primary School, my eldest sister got married. She had completed her schooling and, as was the practice in those days, was married off at an early age.

My mother, Kesabati Mohanta, was not highly educated, but she made up for that by immersing herself in the efficient running of the household. We had several attendants to tend to the fields and household chores, and she strictly supervised them, ensuring that everything was taken care of. She also maintained the earnings from our agricultural produce. I would accompany her to the various weddings we were invited to. I recall one particular incident from 1998. I had returned from IIT-Kharagpur after taking a test and slept off in my room after a long period of studying. When I awoke at four in the morning, I was surprised to see my mother asleep on the floor. When she woke up, I asked her about it. She said she did not want to disturb my sleep, so she lay on the floor. I was deeply touched; only a mother can have such compassion for her child.

Returning to my higher secondary school days, Ravenshaw College in Cuttack was considered among the most prestigious in Odisha. Many of its students went on to have successful careers, either as high-ranking government officials or in other such positions. My father was keen that at least one of his children should be educated at Ravenshaw so he could proudly declare the feat to others. I would later realize his dream.

Getting Serious about Studies

I was an average student to begin with and did not take my studies seriously until the fourth standard. For some reason, I went through a transformation in fifth grade. I became studious. Soon, I was among the top two students in my class. I placed second in the final examinations and secured a scholarship, which propelled me to do even better. There were times when textbooks for some subjects were not available, and I had to copy the content from a friend or peer's book. As I wrote down the passages, I internalized the information, which helped me in the examinations. This came in handy, especially for History, wherein memorizing dates and names was essential. From the sixth until the eighth standard, I consistently finished first in my class examinations.

I did not have to face the struggles that students in villages had, such as a lack of power supply. There was a regular supply of electricity in Jashipur even back then, and it played truant only during the summers. Besides, my sister Damyanti guided me in Math. For a while, I also took tuitions for the subject. I think my love for math developed through those early interactions with Damyanti, now a health worker. She was a pillar of strength for my grandparents and parents. Apart from my grandfather, parents and sister Damyanti, my grandmother, Barini Mohanta, influenced me. She not only took care of her visually impaired husband but also made sure that the household ran in an efficient, clockwork manner.

My father's interest in my studies was primarily focused on my performance in Math. So long as I did well in that subject, he was satisfied, and not bothered about my marks in other subjects. Of course, I was not allowed to fail in them. As an incentive, my father announced that if I scored more than 90 per cent in Math, he would give me the pocket money I desired. I obliged, and in return, I got a tidy amount of close to 25 paise every week, which I spent on various pursuits, particularly sweets. I supplemented this income by selling kids' stickers (which I would secure from a store outside Jashipur) to my school friends. The stickers would be pasted on book covers to make them look attractive.

My father also treated me to *aloo-chop* and *rasagolla* from the local Kaptan Hotel. Because he avoided eating in restaurants, we would get the delicacy packed and devour it by a pond filled with clean water close to our place. Many lessons that have helped me build a successful life came from my father: discipline, dedication, self-confidence and never to give up even in the face of formidable challenges.

I used to sleep by eight in the night and wake up by four in the morning because my grandfather and father would be up at the crack of dawn to discuss and plan for the day's work. That habit remained with me for years, helping me in my studies. To this day, I try to remain an early riser, though I must admit that due to my current engagements, it has become difficult to stick to this plan.

I would often go to the fields before school and help my father and the attendants. I learned to plough the fields and drive bullock carts, a couple of which we owned. I would drive the cart to the nearby forest to collect firewood. During the summer vacations, I became a full-time farmer by default.

I still recall how big an occasion it was when a local resident purchased a bus, which was named Ashirwaad; it was the first such purchase in our town. There was a grand puja in the nearby Kichakeswari Devi Temple at Khiching organized by the proud bus owner. I bunked school with a few friends to attend the event. Our class teacher, Ms Radha Panda, was a disciplinarian and was not amused by our actions. We had a tough time placating her.

I remember another incident from my early school days. In the seventh grade, we used to have what was called the NRTS (National Rural Talent Search) examinations. Just before the test, I was struck by malaria and typhoid and was admitted to a local hospital. I was the first patient there with the disease combo and was quarantined in a room, with people working in shifts outside the room to keep an eye on me. The blessings of my family and friends and the dedication of the medical staff helped me recover.

When I was in the sixth grade, I participated in a unique event organized by the school. It was called the Arithmetic Race, in which students of sixth, seventh and eighth grades participated. We had to run 100 metres, solve a mathematical problem on a board at the other end and run back. I won that competition despite the presence of seventh- and eighth-standard students in the race.

Like many school boys, I enrolled in the Scouts programme, soon becoming a leader. Scouts training further inculcated in me the importance of discipline and generated an interest in social service. The other event I successfully participated in was a quiz contest. I used to read numerous books on general knowledge, which proved useful. I won the contest at the school level and then topped the competition at the district level.

Although still a young boy, I was always on the lookout for opportunities to secure my future. In those days, there used to be a professional examination, Bandani, to select teachers to teach Hindi in government schools. I took that examination on a whim and cleared it. Now I had a backup plan for a professional career. In case nothing else worked out, I could get a job as a Hindi teacher in Odisha!

World Beyond Jashipur

My passing the eighth grade with flying colours was a joyous occasion for my family and friends, but it also came with heartbreak. My brother suggested that I move out for further studies and said that I should shift to his place in Purnapani near Rourkela. He argued that I needed to broaden my horizons. Mahesh's views were always held in high regard. He was the first member of our family from the paternal side to get a corporate job. He was right, of course, but it meant that I had to bid goodbye to Jashipur, my parents and my friends, even if for only two years. It was a tough but necessary call for a bright future. Thus began a new phase of my life.

I went to live with my brother in Purnapani in Sundargarh district, some 40 km away from the steel city of Rourkela and was enrolled in Ispat High School, managed by the Steel Authority of India Limited (SAIL). I soon realized that I had been like a frog in a well who thinks that the well is the whole world. Jashipur had been my world, and I had not imagined anything existed beyond it. Today, the entire world is in one's drawing room through television sets but there was no TV back then.

In my new school, I was faced with students who came from urban backgrounds, could speak better English, dressed smartly and discussed various topics that I had no understanding of. It was a kind of culture shock for me. The teachers were different, too. In Jashipur, the teachers behaved well with me, treating me with care and compassion. Here, barring a few exceptions, they were largely impersonal. I felt that among the students and teachers, I was considered a second-class citizen, a village boy! Needless to say, I had enormous trouble adjusting to the new environment. At times, I despaired, wondering if I would ever fit into the new system.

The qualities my father had inculcated in me had made me resilient. Help also came from an unexpected source. I met a teacher my brother knew, and he offered to tutor me. Slowly but surely, I began to regain my confidence. I did well in the ninth standard, although I failed to top my class. Looking back, I believe that the marks given by the teachers in some subjects were less than what I deserved and that the teachers were prejudiced against me but I could do nothing about it. Instead, I resolved to work harder. I was weak in

Sanskrit and English. My school headmaster, Remish Lakra, was a kind soul. Sensing my discomfort and perhaps noticing my untapped potential, he decided to offer me extra classes without charging a paisa. I greatly benefitted from his efforts and did not disappoint him. I worked extra hard to ensure that I neutralized the disadvantages I had come with.

After the 10th-grade examinations were over—the examination centre was in Birmitrapur—I returned to Jashipur, happy to be reunited with my family and friends. While I waited for the results, I indulged in my old pastimes: swimming in the pond, ploughing the fields, driving the bullock carts and plucking and eating raw mangoes rubbed with salt. I assured my parents that I had done well.

This was in mid-1986. Weeks after my return, I received the news from my brother that I had not only passed but also topped my school. The even more exhilarating news was that I was among the toppers in all of Odisha! This ranking was like the proverbial icing on the cake. I also received the Nehru Memorial Award for academic excellence from the Rourkela Steel Plant.

Everyone was happy, but my father was happiest; he was in seventh heaven because his dream was about to be realized. Buoyed by my academic performance and prodded by my father, I applied to Ravenshaw College in Cuttack, and my application was accepted. In those days, 11th- and 12th-grade studies were conducted by the college. I also received an offer from a leading college in Bhubaneswar, Buxi Jagabandhu Bidyadhar (BJB), but there were limited hostel facilities. In any case, my father was determined that I study at Ravenshaw, and it was my first choice, too. It was one of the state's top colleges. Now, it is a university. However, there was an immediate challenge: securing admission to the hostel. Only 30 seats were vacant, but because of my high marks, I managed to gain a place in the hostel. Only the brightest students could secure admission to that hostel, which was among the biggest in the state. I was ready to take my first big plunge into academics and big-city life.

I arrived in Cuttack. It was the first big city I saw. Now, it would be my home for two years. The shift was not easy. I had to leave my beloved Jashipur, family and friends and meet complete strangers. Education was imparted in English, my weak spot. The adjustment here was far more difficult than it had been in Purnapani, where I had my brother's support and presence. This was a real city, some 200 km from Jashipur, and I was a small-town boy uncomfortable with the general environment. One of my cousins, Pancheswar Mohanta, accompanied me because he had been to Cuttack before for his law examination and knew the city. He returned after I had settled down.

I had no one to give me moral support. I felt alone and was lonely but was determined not to let my father down. I opted for science, but I was weak in Biology. I just could not get the drawings of morphology and the anatomy of plants and animals right. Because it was a subject I could not avoid (I had kept a medical career as an option), I resolved to pass it somehow and concentrate on my strengths, which were Physics, Math and Chemistry. My first-year grades were average, which was not surprising because I was still struggling to acclimatize to an alien environment.

I felt the need to take tuition but could not afford the high cost, so I studied by myself throughout. While I could manage the hostel fees and cost of books with ₹300, the tuition fee alone for Physics and Math was a whopping ₹500–₹600. My hostel mate was Umakant Padhi from Keonjhar, and we studied together because even he could not afford the high tuition fees. My other roommates were my seniors Bijay Sethi and Bhabani Jena, both of whom I am still in touch with.

Hostel life was fun. On Sundays, students would gather around the television set and watch *Ramayan* and *Mahabharat*. It was also a day for a special feast in the hostel mess; mutton would be served, and there would be a long line of students elbowing their way to get a seat at the table. Breakfast was normally puffed rice and *chiwda* powder that I had got from home. At times, when I had spare money, I would step out of the campus for a treat; a Malabar restaurant that served spicy south Indian food was my favourite. When the mess was shut for holidays, my friends and I would visit the Malgoddam region (a wholesale food grain market) for lunch and dinner.

Somehow, I managed to grapple with the problems of studies without tuition and wrote my 12th-grade examinations. I returned home immensely relieved. Before that, in 1988, I watched the Aamir Khan-starrer *Qayamat Se Qayamat Tak* (QSQT) with a friend, who had claimed to have seen it a dozen times already. QSQT was already a blockbuster and went on to become an iconic film, and I greatly enjoyed the experience of watching it in a proper theatre.

Back home, after hearing of my experiences, my father was not hopeful of a good performance. He feared that the lure of a big city had had a bad effect on me, that I had lost focus by succumbing to the razzle-dazzle that Cuttack offered. Imagine his surprise when the results came out. I had secured first division thanks to my excellent marks in Math. My results came out in June 1988 during the auspicious Raja Sankranti period.

Those were not the days of online results. A Results Bulletin was issued in Bhubaneswar and circulated in different cities. Resourceful people would get hold of those bulletins and sell them in smaller towns such as ours. One Imtiaz bhai from Jashipur had the bulletin, and I cycled to his residence, which was close by. On seeing that I had passed with a first division, I returned home. I was so happy that I forgot to duck as I entered my house, knocking my head on the low roof. I did not feel anything then, but a few hours later, a blood clot had formed. Thankfully, it healed in a few days.

As I look back at the time I spent in Jashipur and Cuttack, I remember many of my friends, particularly those from my primary school days, Ananta and 'Paltu' Prakash Sahu. I have kept in touch with them through the years and even met them recently. I had other friends, too: Ghana Mohanta, my neighbour and accomplice in several mischievous endeavours, Quila, Bula, Santosh Singh, Vijay Singh, Hati, Jitendra, Debanand, Chiranjib and Ranjit Ram, to name a few.

I cannot but express my gratitude to two of our family's key support staff, Ravi Dehury and Hira Mohakud. Ravi was on guard duty almost the entire day when I had been hospitalized with malaria and typhoid. Hira was my grandfather's Man Friday. He also surreptitiously encouraged me to slip away to see a film and taught me the art of watching the local *jatra* or drama without having to pay the entry fee.

Once again, it was time to look beyond Jashipur for my future. What next after Ravenshaw? And where? The answer to the first question was clear. I had to appear for the JEE examinations to gain entry into one of the prestigious Indian Institutes of Technology (IITs). I began preparing earnestly, referring to various books. I was glad that I could solve the problems in Halliday & Resnick's Fundamentals of Physics, which was considered the best reading material for those aspiring to attend an IIT. The 'why' would be decided depending on whether I got through and which IIT I got.

2
Engineering My Dream

Throughout, my aim had been to join a prestigious engineering college, but by the time I completed the 12th grade, in which I secured a first class, I had missed the dates of the entrance tests for engineering institutions that year. I could do nothing but prepare for the examinations to be held the following year. However, I did not want to waste a year merely studying for the tests, so I decided to enrol in a BSc course at Government College, Rourkela. It was an arts, science and commerce college, and my subjects were Physics, Chemistry and Math (PCM).

Besides not wanting to waste a year, I thought that if I did not make it to an engineering college, I would at least be a graduate and could pursue a decent career. It was the same old desire to have a backup plan, like when I had taken a test to become a Hindi teacher or when I studied Biology to consider a career in medicine.

Rourkela was not new to me. As a class 12 student, I used to travel by road on the Purnapani–Jashipur route via Rourkela. At times, I even visited my cousin sister Jayanti Didi in Rourkela, which was 35 km from Purnapani. I liked the planned city, with its two major rivers, having pleasant weather most of the year. It has two separate townships: the steel township and the civil township. The steel township, comprising the Rourkela Steel Plant and its associated constructions—such as the residential quarters for the plant's employees—is elaborately landscaped with green coverage and artistic structures. I would pass by the township while travelling from Purnapani to Jashipur and back.

My attendance in college was low, meeting the bare minimum days that the college authorities had mandated. It was because my focus was not so much on graduation studies as on clearing the engineering entrance examinations that were due soon. I planned to take three tests: IIT–JEE, Odisha JEE and one for the prestigious Indian School of Mines (ISM) in Dhanbad (then in undivided Bihar, now IIT Dhanbad). I had to take specialized coaching because the 12th standard syllabus was very different from the questions I would encounter in the ISM and IIT–JEE tests; the Odisha JEE paper would, however, be close to what I had studied in the 12th grade of the Council of Higher Secondary Education of the Odisha state.

Like many other students, I opted for the famous Mishra Coaching Centre. I fail to recall the founding tutor's full name, but I do remember that Mishra sir was from Bihar and was an excellent teacher. His methods were such that one could quickly grasp the essentials. His fee was low, and being a simple man, he often did not keep a tab on which students had paid the fee and which students had not. The only problem was that his coaching centre was at least 15 km away from the hostel I stayed in. I rode my bicycle the full distance and back. On rare occasions, I would get a lift on a motorcycle or moped from another student. Because I had to attend college later in the day, I would set out from my hostel at 4.30 a.m. for the 6 a.m. classes, then return to the hostel and get ready for college. The early morning travel was taxing and uncomfortable, especially in the biting winter season. Besides, at that time, the stretch of road was isolated and many students feared that something untoward could happen to them.

Because Mishra sir was so popular, he attracted a large number of students, and the small room in which he ran his coaching business proved woefully inadequate to accommodate us all. Many of us would spread out in the open to take the mock examinations, sitting at suitable distances so that we did not copy from each other! We would take our positions at the bottom of a nearby hill near the Gayatri Temple, which was in front of the famous IG Park, where we would take the mock test that would be evaluated by our peers. Studying like this was fun. Additionally, I took a correspondence course from Agarwal Classes for IIT JEE.

At the hostel, my roommates were Saroj Mohanta and Aichi. I also came across several other students in the hostel whom I knew from my school days or whose relatives I knew.

Getting into a Dream Institute

Sometime in March/April 1989, I appeared for the tests and returned to Jashipur, where again I engaged in agricultural activities while waiting for the results.

While the results for IIT–JEE and Odisha JEE were delayed that year due to some internal issues, the ISM results were declared and I was selected. My family was overjoyed because ISM was a prestigious institution, ranked among the best engineering colleges in the country, and they pressured me to join. I now had to relocate to Dhanbad. I would be going outside Odisha for studies for the first time, but I was enthusiastic, though a bit apprehensive, about leaving my beloved state. With mixed feelings, I proceeded to

Dhanbad with my brother. In those days, there was no direct bus service from Jashipur to Dhanbad, and we had to get down at Jamshedpur for the rest of the journey. The bus was packed with commuters, and I had to travel standing for more than 250 km from Jashipur to Dhanbad. I was tired, but the thrill of joining ISM somehow dulled the pain.

On reaching the ISM campus, I was immediately impressed as it was large, well-equipped and beautifully maintained. It seemed to provide every facility available. The damper, however, was the classrooms. Students had to sit cramped together on small benches, which was troublesome because we hardly had any elbow room. What I learned later was even more troubling. ISM was tough for first-year students as they had to face ragging.

Fortunately, I knew a few senior students and escaped the torture. Even then, to be on the safer side, I spent many nights outside the college hostel along with some classmates to escape ragging, which would eventually play an important part in my decision to quit ISM.

Ragging aside, I had a difficult time adjusting to the institute's environment and was seeking a way out. Fortunately, the opportunity came my way when the Odisha JEE results were announced. I was among the selected students and was asked to appear for counselling in Rourkela. Although the student was counselled along with their parents, my father or other close relatives could not come because my grandfather had recently passed away. I had to decide on my own. Due to my marks, I was assured of admission to other regional engineering colleges (now called the National Institutes of Technology [NITs]) as well.

I went for counselling in June and accepted the offer to join NIT-Rourkela. Getting a seat at the NIT was an achievement. If I remember correctly, there were 360 seats, of which half were kept for students from Odisha. Of those, 50 per cent were reserved for students from SC/ST and other reserved categories. In other words, only around 80 seats were available for general-category students like me. There were private engineering institutes, too, where I could have gained admission, but the best quality higher educational institutions in engineering were government-managed. I became the first student in my family, immediate and extended, to secure admission to an engineering college. I would also go on to become my family's first engineering graduate.

From Rourkela, I went straight to Jashipur and informed my family about my decision. They were aghast that I had chosen to quit ISM. As far as they were concerned, ISM was higher in status than NIT-Rourkela, but I was adamant. Was I glad to have escaped ISM? You bet.

Securing admission to NIT-Rourkela was a dream come true. Most students in Odisha who wished to study engineering in the state hoped to be selected for this prestigious institution. The sprawling campus was wonderful, as were the facilities. For the first time, I believed I could achieve my potential. Besides, my selection also took care of my future. I was assured of a good job once I passed out with good grades; for an NIT-R graduate to not get employment was unheard of. I packed my bags once more and headed to Rourkela, which, by now, had become a second home.

One thing that impressed me most about the curriculum was its emphasis on matching the needs of the industry with the syllabus. There were classes on theory as well as practical exposure and training. In the first year, we were taken to an industrial group every weekend to understand its working at the ground level first-hand. At the end of the year, there were summer visits to an industrial campus. This was a mandatory assignment; none of us wanted to miss it anyway because it gave us the opportunity to travel to new places, meet new people and learn new things. We also interacted with various industry leaders.

I recall the legendary Russi Mody (of the Tata Group) addressing us at the Tata Steel Plant in my first year. What impressed me most when I learned about him in my later years was his ability to spot talent and back that talent with all his might, even when faced with opposition. He was a master at creating a second line of effective leadership; because of this style, after he left, a string of leaders who took up high positions came from within the organization, and they were people he had nurtured and prepared for leadership positions.

Various other industry leaders also occasionally interacted with us. During my time at the Institute, we were also taken to Dalmia's cement plant, Rourkela steel plant, etc., as part of our industry-visit programme. Those visits greatly enhanced our understanding of the industrial sector in a way that only theory classes within the confines of our institute would not have been able to. These interactions helped us broaden our horizons, and in my case, they nurtured dreams of one day becoming an entrepreneur.

The NIT-R course also included classes in Political Science and Economics, which helped us understand the larger issues governing industry. In the Economics classes, we learned about the supply-and-demand phenomenon, among other topics.

There was ragging at NIT, too, but it was not as bad as at ISM. Besides, I escaped it altogether. For the first few days, apprehensive about it, I stayed with my cousin sister, Jayanti Didi. Back in the campus hostel, I was lucky to share a room with two seniors. Because both were some sort of leaders, nobody dared to rag me. As part of the ragging process, freshers were not allowed to use their bicycles to travel from the hostel to the classroom, but nobody stopped me when I did so. Freshers were supposed to dress formally, with proper shoes and everything, but I could wear anything I wanted. I also spoke with my seniors while looking them in the eyes, which freshers were not permitted to do. All in all, I had a good time.

My four years at NIT-Rourkela passed smoothly, though there was one challenge: the fees had gone up to ₹500–600 per month. I had to manage somehow with the scholarship amount I had been receiving and with some money my brother gave me. Otherwise, I studied hard and did well in the examinations. At the same time, I enjoyed watching films with my friends. Our campus had an audiovisual hall where films were screened, and we would gather there to relax. The films were chosen by third-year students, and at times, they selected films I was not particularly keen on. In such cases, I simply skipped the screening.

In the summer of 1991, I visited the Coal India Limited unit in Nagpur with other students. It was terribly hot, and I was not used to such temperatures. For the first time in my life, I saw people using air coolers. It was difficult for me to manage, but I did so, thinking all the time that one had to face challenges if one wanted to achieve something meaningful in life. I took it as one more new experience in my life.

In Nagpur, we stayed at the Graduate Engineering Trainee (GET) Hostel. Students had come from different parts of the country, belonging to various engineering colleges. GET hostels are located in various places. I stayed at the GET facility when I visited the Tata Steel Plant, too. Many students were struck by jaundice and had to cut their stay short and return home. Thankfully, I was spared, though I was so tired that when I returned home, I took some much-needed rest, which rejuvenated me. In my third year at NIT-Rourkela, we visited Hindustan Copper Limited's facility at Ghatsila, not far from Jamshedpur.

In my fourth year, I was part of several industry visits, this time to Mumbai, Goa and Bangalore. We always took the train, and although we were not travelling in the comforts of first class, we enjoyed the trips. In Goa, we visited the Sesa Goa (engaged in mining and other businesses) facilities and the National Institute of Oceanography. In Mumbai, we went to the Aditya Birla Group headquarters and a research institute in Colaba. We visited the facilities of Hindustan Aeronautics Limited (HAL) and Bharat Earth Movers Limited (BEML) in Bangalore.

During that year, I also began preparing for the GRE and MBA entrance tests. By then, I had started thinking big and believed that if an opportunity came my way to study in the US, I should grab it. For that, I had to pass the GRE. My English, written and spoken, was weak. Not too far from the NIT campus was a small coaching centre that taught spoken English. I joined it and attended classes twice a week. I cannot say that my English became remarkably fluent, as it was for those who studied it since kindergarten, but there was some improvement. While preparing for the GRE, I worked on my written English a great deal, learning many new words and phrases. I was quite delighted by the improvement.

At NIT, I always had trouble framing questions in English because I thought in Odiya and then tried to mentally translate it into English, so I hesitated to ask my professors any questions. Similarly, I would fumble while replying in

English, even when I knew the answers. I suppose this is an issue for many students across the country whose first language is not English and who took to the language later in school. It is a challenge, but it cannot be allowed to come in the way of one's progress.

I somehow managed the handicap, but if I were to go to the US, my level of English would be woefully inadequate. I had also begun studying for CAT to gain admission to the top Indian Institutes of Management (IIMs). Here, too, proficiency in English was needed to cross the group discussion and interview hurdles.

While doing all this, I kept in mind that I might not, at that stage, join an MBA programme even if I made it to the shortlist of candidates because the fee was way too prohibitive for me; it ran into lakhs even back then. Coaching was also expensive. Still, I saw no harm in preparing for the exams. At the very least, the preparation would help me learn more and be ready for future opportunities.

I did not take the GRE test, though I did well in the mock interview conducted before the test. I sat for a separate entrance test for Xavier's Institute of Management (XIM), Bhubaneswar, as well as for XLRI. I got through XIM but decided not to sit for the group discussion and interview rounds because I had no money to meet the cost of study and felt it was a waste of time and energy to appear for the selection rounds.

While my academic performance in my first year at NIT was average, I was among the top five students in the subsequent years, scoring more than 65 per cent consistently, which was considered fairly high in those days. I believed that even without going to the US immediately or doing an MBA, I could make some headway in my career. The immediate need was a job, and my family wholeheartedly agreed with my view. I consoled myself saying that I could do an MBA after getting a job and saving some money.

It was 1993, and the economic reforms undertaken by the P.V. Narasimha Rao government had begun showing results. Suddenly, the industrial sector opened up and the licence-permit-quota raj came to a crashing end. While the Indian corporate sector was happy with the development, it had to adjust to meet the new challenges that came with liberalization. Thus, for the short term, Indian corporates cut down on hiring, and the job market was down.

Through campus interviews, I was among the ones shortlisted by Tata Steel. I lost out narrowly as the company decided to take just one student from our batch, and I was second on the list. I then appeared for a job interview for another private mining company, Ferro Alloys Corporation Limited. The mined product was treated and transported to Paradip Port and then it made its way to foreign markets.

Here, too, I placed second. The first-placed candidate would have got the job, and I would have lost out yet again, but providence came to my rescue. When the first-placed candidate was told by the interview panel that he would have to sign a bond, he dithered, saying he would have to seek advice from his father. I was eager not to let the opportunity slip out of my hands and expressed instant willingness to sign the document, which would bind me to the company for a certain number of years. Later, the panel members sarcastically told the first candidate that he could keep asking for advice from his father, grandfather and others, while the company gave the job to another candidate.

Needless to say, I was excited. Ferro Alloys Corporation Limited produces high carbon ferro chrome and is reputed for its quality products and services in the domestic as well as global markets.

That is how I landed my first job. I would be based near Bhadrak, around 150 km from Bhubaneswar. The salary was around ₹2,700 per month. It wasn't much, but the company provided accommodation and a vehicle to pick up and drop off the employees, thus saving me money on rent and travel.

I had returned to Jashipur when the appointment letter came. I was poised to begin a new phase of my life.

3
When Work Is Fun

I was ecstatic when the appointment letter from Ferro Alloys Corporation arrived. I was especially happy for my family because their efforts to get me educated and the trust they had reposed in my abilities had finally paid off. I was glad that I had not let them down. As for my father, I cannot even explain the delight he felt.

Before I proceeded to Bhadrak to join work, I had to make one important trip. So off we went—my parents, sisters, brother and several other members of my extended family—to Ma Tarini Temple, located some 80 km from Jashipur. We paid our obeisance to the family deity, thanking her for her benevolence and praying that we continue to receive her patronage.

I joined Ferro Alloys as a graduate engineer trainee. It was an officer-grade post given to engineering graduates; diploma-holders were absorbed as workers. As a trainee officer, I had access to several benefits. I could use the officers' mess where the food was good and available at a nominal price; I was given decent, fully-furnished accommodation; I could relax in the company club environs that were equipped with many recreational facilities. Our residential campus was at some distance from the office and had all the basic amenities. Needless to say, I thoroughly enjoyed the many privileges.

My office was in Boula, near Bhadrak. As part of the training, I was given stints in all the departments: accounts, administration, human resources, the shop floor, inventory, sales, etc. Along with the other graduate engineer trainees, I worked in the morning and evening shifts; the night shifts were for non-officers. The exposure helped me gain a holistic understanding of the company's functioning and at least a basic knowledge of the activities of the various departments. I learned the importance of the synergy needed to make a company stand out from the rest.

We worked hard through the weekdays, whereas the weekends were for leisure. The company provided us with vehicles, and I would often use the facility to visit my family in Jashipur or go to a nearby city to watch a film.

My immediate superior was a wonderful person named Nandagiri Veera, who now lives in the US. Originally from Hyderabad, he was born and raised in Bihar. A deputy general manager-level official, he took a liking to me. At times, I was late to work because the vehicle that came to pick up the trainees from home was running behind schedule. I would quietly slip into my seat, but somehow, Mr Veera knew I had arrived late. In fact, he had the exact information about everybody. One day, he called me and asked what I would do after getting that month's salary. I looked at him nonplussed. He gently suggested that I could consider purchasing a bicycle, adding with a mischievous look that I would then report to work on time. I got the message.

Work and Fun

During breaks, we would occasionally slip into the nearby posh guest house to relax. Veera sir would learn of that, too, without leaving his chair. He had a great network of informants. Though he wondered what we did in the guest house, he never took us to task. Not once during my tenure with the company did he scold me for any reason. He treated his subordinates with care and concern, and this made us give our best.

Our general manager was the late Mr M.K. Pujari, who was Veera's immediate boss. Trainees like us hardly had any reason to interact with him. He had a reputation for being strict and aggressive, so we did not even have any desire to reach out to him. He had been a topper at IT-BHU (now IIT-BHU) and ran his department with total control. I later learned that Pujari was from Odisha. This came as a surprise to me because Odiya people are gentle and generally not known for belligerence. Perhaps the fact that he had spent most of his career outside the state had shaped his attitude.

I would probably not have interacted with him but for a sudden turn of events. Ferro Alloys Corporation decided to collaborate with IIT-Kharagpur on a project related to rock mechanics and ventilation.

One day, I was summoned by the big boss himself. It is possible that Mr Pujari had heard about me from Mr Veera. I walked into the general manager's office with trepidation. My first impression of him confirmed everything I had heard about him. He was stern, with hardly a smile on his face. Because I was meeting him for the first time, I thought he would put me at ease, but he came straight to the point and asked for my input. In those days, I used to read a lot about factory and mine mechanization and had updated knowledge about rock mechanics and ventilation/ fluid mechanics. I gave him my views and later made a presentation on the topic.

Apparently, he was pleased because, after that first meeting, he called me into his chamber numerous times, seeking my opinion on other issues regarding the company's functioning. Soon, word spread that I had a special relationship with him. Every time I emerged from his office, my colleagues would crowd around me to ask what had been discussed. The good part about this development was that I suddenly became an important person in the organization and my colleagues began respecting me more. I enjoyed the attention, but it also meant that I had more responsibility to bear. The key learning from this was to never be complacent and to remain updated with the latest trends in your field. Doing so helped me get that recognition.

I was relieved to see the close of my first year with the firm because, for the first twelve months, we were not entitled to any paid leave. Every time I took a leave, I lost ninety rupees for each day of absence. From the second year onwards, I would get paid leave. After my training period, I was also promoted to the post of assistant manager.

Although I was now an engineer, my old dream of doing an MBA continued to simmer. I hadn't been able to pursue that dream because of financial constraints, but now I believed I could afford it. Meanwhile, knowing that I was interested in finance, somebody suggested I appear for the Chartered Financial Analyst (CFA) examination. It was a difficult test to clear, and the first part involved getting through the Diploma in Business Finance (DBF). I joined a correspondence course offered by the Institute of Chartered Financial Analysts of India (ICFAI), which was newly established in 1994, and attended classes once or twice a week in Cuttack, taking paid leaves for the purpose. Although the DBF was a one-year course, it took me longer to clear because of time constraints.

As an assistant manager, my salary had increased to ₹4,200 a month, but my responsibilities had also increased because I had independent charge of a few functions. I had clerical staff in my team, some of whom were diploma holders, trained at Indian Technical Institutes (ITIs). I could now, for the first time, invest in an LIC policy and other tax-saving measures. I served as an assistant manager for close to two years, and it was fun and a great learning experience. I had a part-time maid to take care of household chores; her remuneration was taken care of by the company. I also had a company vehicle on a shared basis at my disposal.

In 1994, my youngest sister, Damyanti, got married. I contributed to the expenses, though not as much as I wanted. I took out a loan of ₹20,000 from a private money lender, bought her a gold necklace worth ₹12,000, and used the balance for other wedding expenses. I repaid the loan over five months. I was delighted to have helped my family.

My next promotion was as manager in 1996. I visited Jashipur once a month on the weekends using the company jeep. I would start early in the morning on a Sunday—the journey took three-and-a-half hours one way; now, the distance can be covered in under three hours because the roads have become better—and return late that same evening. After my sister Damyanti moved to her husband's place, my parents lived alone and looked forward to my trips.

There was another wedding in my family—my eldest sister's daughter, Pinki's marriage—after I became a manager. She had been taking care of my parents and was much loved by everyone. This time, I could contribute substantially. My elder brother could not make it to the event because he had been transferred to Madhya Pradesh and was busy with work at the new place.

While preparing for the three-year CFA course, I realized that I could not find adequate time to study while being employed. I decided to quit and concentrate on not only the CFA but also the MBA. Even then, I could not afford the fees of IIT-Kharagpur (roughly ₹75,000), which conducted a Master's course in Business Management. Meanwhile, to boost my career prospects, I also appeared for the FCC Metal First Class Mines examination. In those days, there was a great demand for mine managers, and those with the FCC certification were preferred. My old habit of having a Plan B kicked in, and I took the examination. Not only did I clear it but I also became the youngest Indian, at the age of 26, to do so. The certification added value to my profile and fetched a slightly higher salary of around ₹6,000 per month.

However, an FCC-certified engineering graduate commanded a far higher salary in those days, it was around ₹15,000 per month. I had to decide whether to continue my present job and hope for small incremental hikes in salary (which would push my hopes of doing an MBA further into the future) or quit and look for a position elsewhere where I could get the money I needed for the purpose. The second option appealed to me, and I began looking for an opening. I found an advertisement that announced a vacancy at Hindustan Aluminium Company (Hindalco). It was for a senior position and required work experience of at least eight years. I did not have that kind of experience, but I applied nonetheless.

I also faced some other challenges. The company (Ferro Alloys) was hit by labour unrest after a standoff between the management and workers, who were represented by their labour union. A second challenge was worker management within the team. I was young, in a leadership position and had several people older than me who had to work under my supervision. I realized that giving people the respect they deserve, listening to their suggestions and readily accepting those that are good for the organization helped win over their trust and confidence. I had to appreciate that the employees came from different states, had different approaches and spoke different languages, though Hindi was the link language. Once I realized this, it became easier for me to relate to them and my task of management became less difficult.

Everyone liked my emphasis on ensuring complete safety standards. It was a learning experience for me to meet daily and monthly targets and ensure that all safety precautions, rules and regulations were strictly adhered to.

In those days, Hindalco did not have a big presence in Odisha. It had facilities in Ranchi and Sambalpur. G.C. Mittal was in charge of the operations. The company had big plans. The first round of interviews was held in Bhubaneswar. Mittal wasn't there. I crossed that hurdle and prepared for the final round to be conducted in Ranchi. I later learned that Mittal was impressed by the fact that I had cleared the FCC test at such a young age. He sought advice from S.N. Padhi, the then Director General of Mines Safety (DGMS), who apparently gave positive feedback about me. I did well in the final interview round, where I was asked several practical questions. Because I had worked on the ground, I gave the correct and practical replies. Thus, waiving the condition of eight years of experience, Mittal announced that the company would hire me. I returned to Bhadrak elated.

The Hindalco Experience

I got the offer letter, left Ferro Alloys after working there for a little over four years, and joined Hindalco in October 1997 as a manager with a salary far higher than my previous one at Ferro Alloys. The job was tough but satisfying. I was based in Ranchi but had to travel to two other company sites, one being Lohardaga. Naxals were very active in that region in those days, and for safety, I would stay overnight at one of the sites rather than risk travelling late in the evenings back to Ranchi.

Now, with a better salary and the possibility of saving some money, I was within striking distance of securing an MBA. I applied to XIM-Bhubaneswar and IIT-Kharagpur for a Master's in Business Management. I eventually chose the latter because the cost of studying at XIM was nearly two lakh rupees, while at IIT, it was ₹75,000. Barely six months after joining Hindalco, I resigned to pursue my Master's.

I had long been preparing hard for the entrance test, joining a correspondence course at the IMS. I also attended classes in Cuttack to prepare for the group discussion and interview while working for Hindalco. After clearing the test, I faced the interview panel.

One of the interviewers was an expert in supply chain management, a topic I had come well-prepared for. I did not know then that he was close to Russi Mody and J.J. Irani, another stalwart of Tata Steel. He did consultancy work for the Tata Group and was close to Mr Irani. The interviewer's name was Professor D. Acharya. Later, I discovered that he was from Odisha. I did not know then that he was from my college, NIT-Rourkela, and from my home district, too. He asked me the most questions at the interview. Later, I would top his classes at IIT in Supply Chain. He is retired now and settled in Odisha, and I make it a point to meet him whenever I visit the state. He is still my mentor and guide.

Amidst these developments, I suffered a personal blow. My father died of a cardiac arrest in 1998 on Rama Navami. He had been a pillar of strength throughout my life, encouraging me to study as much as I wanted and pursue whatever career I chose. He never allowed the family's financial constraints to come in the way of me realizing my dreams. He was the one person in the family who backed my decision to give up a good job to pursue an MBA; others had discouraged me, pointing out that I was taking a huge risk by giving up a high-paying job. Looking back, the only consolation I can derive is that he lived to see me succeed.

Having said goodbye to Hindalco, I arrived in Kharagpur and was back on an educational campus and hostel life. The transition wasn't easy. I had been working full-time for close to five years in senior managerial positions, but now, I was just another student. I had to adjust my temperament. Besides, I was no longer getting a salary at the end of the month.

The fact that I was finally pursuing a course at an IIT, a dream I had nurtured for years, was satisfying. Initially, I struggled financially. While the hostel and facilities were of high quality—I had my own room with marble flooring—the cost was high, too, but I managed somehow.

During those challenging days, I had support from a few classmates, who had also left their jobs and joined the institute for their Master's. They would laughingly say that it was a do-or-die situation for all of us and we had to emerge victorious. The moral support we gave one another helped us a lot in times of self-doubt.

Kharagpur was a little away from the city, but there were good restaurants and film theatres nearby. I travelled by cycle rickshaws from our campus to this 'happening' place. Jamshedpur and Kolkata were the nearest big cities. During my first year at the IIT, I went on industrial visits to both these cities with other students.

At the close of the first semester, our seniors told us that the finance sector was undergoing a rough phase and that there weren't many job openings in that field. Instead, the information technology (IT) sector was booming. I had to decide whether to continue with my decision to specialize in finance or shift gears. My father was no longer there, and the responsibility of the family was on me. I had to make sure I got a well-paying job after my studies. Not wanting to take any chances, I switched to Systems/IT.

The last six months at IIT were for internships. I interned with the leading IT firm, HCL, in Kolkata. I stayed at the company's guest house in Salt Lake, one of the city's posh regions, during my internship. My performance was appreciated. Upon returning to the Institute, I made a presentation on 'MIS in government accounting'. HCL's Kolkata head, Mr Mazumdar, was among our guides during the internship, and he was always very helpful towards interns.

At the end of the final term, it was time for campus selections. Among the companies that came were HCL and PricewaterhouseCoopers (PwC). I was shortlisted by both, and my inclination was towards PwC; besides the work profile, their salary was also attractive. I guess most shortlisted candidates had it as their first choice. HCL had come for campus selection for the first time, and our coordinator, one of our professors, did not want them to leave empty-handed or with less meritorious students. He asked me to opt for HCL. I had no option but to accept his request.

The year 2000 brought a red-letter day for me when I attended the graduation convocation.

Thus, I began my career with HCL in 2000.

4

Leading from the Front

In May 2000, I began my stint with the leading software solutions firm, HCL, in Kolkata. I had work experience and a management degree, so I did not have to begin as an apprentice; instead, I joined as a consultant in what was seen as a lateral entry.

I was in for a shock when I joined. The company had revised its salary offer southwards, explaining that the IT sector was facing challenging times. Thus, I had to settle for a cost to the company (CTC) of roughly ₹2.2 lakh per annum. After deductions, I received some ₹14,000 per month. This was around the same amount I had been receiving in employment before my MBA.

The offer was relatively better for those who had been absorbed into the company's hardware department, but I was in the software division. I had no option but to accept it. I was told by way of consolation that the salary would be substantially revised after one year; the company kept that promise. In the second year, my salary nearly doubled. The other bright spot was that the job was satisfying, as I got to learn a lot of new things, meet new people and work in leadership positions.

Career in Software

For a few days after joining HCL, I stayed at the company's guest house in Salt Lake City, Kolkata. It is an upmarket, planned satellite city within Kolkata and is home to several leading software firms and high-end residences. The then Chief Minister Jyoti Basu's residence was also in Salt Lake City, and it was not far from where I stayed. After a few days, I moved to a paying guest accommodation close by in an area popularly known as Baisakhi.

Our office, not too far away, was in the Webel SDF Building. The number of employees in the Kolkata unit was small—around a hundred people working primarily on domestic projects. Within a week of joining, I was assigned a project that HCL had signed with IIT-Kharagpur. I was chosen for various reasons: my work experience, my degree, and most of all because I had studied at the IIT and had some understanding of its functioning. IIT-K and HCL were jointly developing software to electronically manage the provident fund accounts of public-sector employees. I made IIT-Kharagpur my base till the completion of the assignment, after which I returned to Kolkata. It was great to return to my alma mater, even if for a brief period. I was there for nearly six months, shuttling between Kharagpur and Kolkata.

While the work environment at HCL was good and the job energizing, I was pretty much on my own, having no support staff or a vehicle at my disposal. I had got used to those perks at my earlier jobs and was now missing them.

During the first year, we had a scare. Our seniors, based in Noida, told us in a meeting that the IT sector was going through tough times and there may be layoffs in departments that were not performing well. One senior executive even said that if the company believed the potato business would fetch profits, HCL would go into potatoes. Humour aside, it was all very unnerving for us. I was fearful. I had just landed a job and had to shoulder familial responsibilities. I could not afford to lose the job. Fortunately, the axe did not fall on me, and I survived.

In fact, I not only survived but also got bigger and more challenging assignments wherein I held leadership positions. HCL had several projects ongoing in India and abroad. In the latter part of 2000, I was chosen by the company to visit Malaysia. Before that, I made a business trip to Chennai. In those days, we made business visits by train or bus, and one had to get special clearance from the top bosses for an air journey. Since my trip was urgent, I got the clearance; thus, for the first time in my life, I sat in an aircraft.

In the years to come, I would travel by air on multiple occasions (I have lost count of them now), but that first journey was special and memorable. I sat glued to my seat, a bit confused and initially uncomfortable, and watched with fascination and some trepidation as the plane took off and then when it landed.

The thrill of that first experience, not only the journey but also the time spent at the airport, cannot be replicated. My thoughts went back to the days I had spent ploughing the fields and driving bullock carts in Jashipur. Now, I was travelling by plane. Had my father been around, he would have been so proud of me. The other thing I still recall is I met the well-known journalist Rajdeep Sardesai on the flight.

My first trip abroad was in the last quarter of 2000. I was asked to visit Malaysia and give a presentation to the Royal Malaysia Police at their headquarters in Kuala Lumpur. I still remember that experience. The city had tall and imposing buildings, the likes of which I had not seen back home. The Royal Malaysia Police was an IT-savvy force, and it was looking for software solutions to streamline its functioning and make it more efficient and transparent.

When a citizen came with a complaint, the case would be registered online. It would then be directed to the relevant team depending on the nature of the crime; it was called case management. The case would be queued up and assigned to an officer, who would pursue and solve it with their core team.

Computerizing the process would mean that the top brass of the police department could monitor case progress on their computer screens and order corrective measures, if necessary. Moreover, even the complainant could track the progress the police force was making. It was a sort of management information system (MIS) the Malaysian police wanted to install. My team and I explained the concept and, after getting the approval, returned to Kolkata, where our software professionals got cracking on the assignment.

In Malaysia, I made an important purchase: a Motorola mobile phone. In those days, even incoming calls were charged, for which the rates were pretty steep. I kept the phone in my bag. Even after returning to India, I used it sparingly. To avoid paying large sums for incoming calls, I gave my number to only a handful of people, including my family members.

My next trip abroad was to Singapore in 2001 to study the loan approval and disbursal system so that a computerized solution could be developed to speed up the process and introduce more transparency. The bank concerned was a major institution in Singapore and Malaysia. The services included personal loans, corporate loans, letters of credit, etc. I made my pitch based on the bank's requirements and returned to Kolkata. However, the bank kept changing the parameters, which made it difficult for us to finalize the solution. Eventually, we managed, thanks to the efforts of our team, especially our salesperson, Debashish Sen.

I made a few purchases in Singapore, too, becoming the proud owner of a Sony double-decker sound system and a Yashica camera.

By then, seniors at HCL had concluded that I had gained expertise in the banking system. This was not true but the impression stuck. Consequently, I was given several assignments related to the banking sector. A senior executive based in Chennai was key in getting me involved with those assignments. By then, the IT sector was booming in India, and major players such as Tata Consultancy Services (TCS) and Infosys had emerged. HCL's top brass concluded that with the domestic market getting crowded and increasingly competitive, the company should look for more business abroad. Bangladesh was one such destination. HCL already had a joint venture with a system integration company there. HCL assigned one person with me on an exclusive basis for support in Dhaka, Bangladesh.

We did a great deal of brainstorming in Chennai regarding the road ahead. Thereafter, I proceeded to Bangladesh. I took a short flight from Kolkata to Dhaka. As soon as I stepped out of the airport, I felt I had landed in Kolkata—the same sort of crowd, chaos, noise, vehicles honking loudly and speeding, and people jostling for space on the roads in a terrifying manner. Even the weather was the same. We had a product in mind and needed to test it in some banks that were interested in it—the First Security Bank, Janata Bank and Sonali Bank. I made many friends there, some of whom I am still in touch with.

Key Personnel

I must acknowledge certain people at HCL who were responsible for my success in the organization. Our head was Dipankar Sengupta, a senior executive whom we addressed as Dipankar *da*. He was a down-to-earth person and extremely knowledgeable about his work. Then there was Kalyan Mazumdar, whom I knew from earlier because he was one of my interviewers for the job. Other senior managers who helped me immensely were Drupad Basu and Ashim Banerjee.

I also came across an interesting person, Arindam Mukhopadhyay, who was the quality control head. He was extremely diplomatic. Over the course of my work, I gradually developed a close bond with him. Interestingly, many years later, after I had branched out on my own, he approached me for a job because he was going through financial difficulties. I accommodated him in my organization. He served for a couple of years as a consultant.

While my professional life was moving steadily, there was action on the personal front too. I was nearing 30 years of age, and my family members were eager for me to marry and settle down. They had already activated the extensive network they had developed over the years to find a suitable bride. My brother, sisters and brothers-in-law plunged into the task of scouting for a girl, and I was left with no choice but to consent to their desire. I was not too finicky about my choice, except that the bride should be well-educated, at least a graduate. I believed such a bride would fit with my education and job profile.

Finding a graduate bride from our caste and community in those days was not an easy task. Other parameters, such as the family's background, also had to be met. On the weekends when I could take time off, I would join my family on visits to the shortlisted families. This went on for some time with no result. Then we were told of a girl in Rairangpur who was a graduate and came from a sound, middle-class family.

Getting Married

I paid an unscheduled visit to the house with a few family members. The girl's family was taken aback by our sudden appearance. A second, planned visit was scheduled thereafter. I met Jaysree who, after her graduation, was teaching in a nursery school, and our two families bonded well. We liked the girl and her family, and they too found us acceptable. The marriage was agreed upon and a date was fixed. My father-in-law had retired from government service and is well-regarded in his area.

I was married on 9 December 2001. The wedding was an elaborate affair, held over three days in Rairangpur and Jashipur. More than six hundred people attended the ceremony. Needless to say, it was an expensive affair. Fortunately, around that time, I had received a tidy sum from HCL by way of some arrears and a salary increment, a good part of which was consumed by the wedding expenses.

Jaysree and I planned a short trip to Puri to pay obeisance at the famous Jagannath Temple. However, the trip had to be cancelled because a distant relative and a neighbour passed away, and as per custom, we could not visit any temple for a certain number of days. Nevertheless, we did go to Cuttack for two days—you can call it a honeymoon—and spent some quality time together. It was her first trip to Cuttack, and we roamed around, carefully avoiding entering any temple.

I returned to Kolkata and resumed work while my wife

stayed in Jashipur. Now my priority was to get suitable accommodation, and I found one at BC Block in Salt Lake City after a good deal of searching. My wife joined me soon after. Some of my friends there, such as Abhijit Banerjee, had also recently got married, and our families quickly grew close. My other friends were Lingaraj Ray and Prakash Kumar. Those were good days. We went for family picnics, including the annual ones organized by HCL. When my family members (from my and my wife's side) visited us, we frequented spots such as Nicco Park, Victoria Memorial and Belur Math. At times, I took Jaysree to visit NIT-Rourkela and showed her the campus.

She would accompany me on business trips whenever possible; for instance, we went to Dhanbad, where we stayed overnight. The visit was for an ongoing assignment for Coal India Limited (CIL) in collaboration with IIT-K. CIL wanted to streamline its provident fund payment system. In those days, there were no mobile phones or other means of instant communication to resolve these issues. CIL received data from satellites and would then download that data and proceed. It was a time-consuming exercise. Our mandate was to make the process quicker and more accurate. It was an upgrade task.

I remember an incident that had nothing to do with my profession but with my association with the Rashtriya Swayamsevak Sangh (RSS). Near our home in Salt Lake was a park where RSS *shakhas* conducted drills. I had been attracted to the RSS since my college days and had even attended some of their drills. I was deeply impressed by the discipline of the RSS workers, their unwavering commitment to the country and their social work. I began visiting Salt Lake Park and became acquainted with many workers there. They were polite and helpful, and over time, I grew close with some of them; they would visit my home, and we would spend time together, discussing various issues of national importance. I believe my association with the RSS helped me hone my discipline and develop an abiding love for my country.

Those were the days of the Left Front rule in West Bengal, and Jyoti Basu was the chief minister. They had neither any interest nor pride in our religious–spiritual heritage. There wasn't a single temple in Salt Lake. Somehow, RSS drills were permitted. Along with a few other like-minded people, we organized a Jagannath Rath Yatra in Salt Lake, which became an annual affair. I am not sure if the event is still held there.

5

Onwards and Upwards!

I had begun feeling at home at HCL Technologies. Prestigious assignments had come my way; I was learning new things; my bosses were happy with my performance, and the salary was much better than before. On the personal front, I was married and feeling emotionally anchored. At this time came another opening that would propel my career even further and give me an opportunity to experience another metropolitan city and its work culture.

In 2002, HCL acquired a 100 per cent stake in a software development company called Gulf Computers Inc. According to a media release, the buyout was for $9.75 million to be paid in tranches. HCL President Shiv Nadar said that the acquisition was a strategic step forward in the implementation of the company's non-linear growth strategy.[1]

Based in the US, Gulf Computers had two offshore development centres in Mumbai and Bangalore. It provided full life-cycle support for customized application development for business process automation, and its clients included the US government and IT firms such as Oracle, Sun and

---

[1] 'HCL Technologies Buys US Company for $10M', *The Telegraph*, 1 June 2002, https://tinyurl.com/munh2aw2. Accessed on 21 February 2025.

Microsoft. The acquisition would help HCL use its offshore capabilities and infrastructure and, more importantly, extend its range of IT services to Gulf Computers' existing clients.

New Work Culture

Dipankar da, my boss with whom I famously got along, directed me to report to Mumbai on deputation and work on the post-merger integration (PMI). PMI is an essential exercise wherein two companies that have come together exchange information regarding their work culture, activities and best practices. The idea is to create a conducive post-merger environment so that both units work seamlessly in the new set-up. I headed to Mumbai, the country's commercial centre, and worked there for about eight months from May 2002 to January 2003.

The strategic head was Srikanth Sundararajan. He had recently relocated from the US after working there for over 20 years. An IIT graduate who had further studied at Stanford, Srikanth had a brilliant mind. He was very down-to-earth and brought with him an informality that exists in American corporations. He insisted we address him as Srik and not 'sir' as everyone back in the US called him Srik. He and I often had breakfast and lunch together, discussing issues of work and beyond. He encouraged me to offer out-of-the-box ideas, and I do not recall a single instance when he dampened my enthusiasm with negative comments. He was a breath of fresh air because senior executives in the Indian IT industry were often so formal that it was difficult for us to open up to them.

Our office was in Andheri in the Santacruz Electronic Export Processing Zone (SEEPZ), and I had been given accommodation a little distance away in Bhandup. I would travel to work and back either by the state-owned BEST bus or an autorickshaw. Days after I settled down, Jaysree joined me in Mumbai; the cost of her air travel was borne by the company. Like me, she was fascinated by the glitter and glamour of the big city. Although we were at a distance from the heart of Mumbai's happening places, such as Marine Drive, Juhu and Colaba, we found time to occasionally visit those spots and let our hair down. I remember we watched the newly-released film *Devdas*. We also took a few trips to Khandala, Lonavala and Alibaug. Most times, though, our outings were to nearby Powai, where we frequented the Hiranandani shopping centre.

Before she came to Mumbai, I would make frequent trips to Kolkata. Srik was magnanimous enough to sanction my airfare, something HCL managers would never have allowed.

I worked closely on PMI and jointly bid for various projects with two colleagues. During the process, I learned a lot from Surjit Kapoor, our pre-sales head for solutions and proposals. He repeatedly reminded us while making a live pitch that we must be passionately involved, as if we were already working on the project. Surjit was old school, remaining somewhat aloof and stern, but for some reason, he came to like me and I could speak with him more freely than others dared to.

Along the way, I made some good friends: Ramesh, Arti Mehra and Supriya Dutta. Supriya and I had a Rourkela connection. Her father had worked for Rourkela Steel Plant. You may recall that I had won a Jawaharlal Nehru award in academics while at Ispat High School; the certificate had been signed by Supriya's father.

One of our mandates in Mumbai was to achieve the Capability Maturity Model Integration (CMMI) Level 3 quality standards. This model helps organizations streamline their processes for optimum efficiency and productivity and reduce risks in software, product and service development. The standard, initiated by the U.S. Department of Defense, was developed by the Software Engineering Institute at Carnegie Mellon University. We worked hard and achieved the certification. The company celebrated it with a party in a five-star hotel in Mumbai's suburbs. It was a novel experience for me, and I was dragged to the dance floor, where I jigged clumsily for a while.

The work culture was very different from that in Kolkata. It was more professional and forward-looking. Our Kolkata unit had not yet attained the CMMI Level 3 stage. On the weekends, I also had the opportunity to attend the Certified Software Quality Analyst course with a small group of employees. It greatly helped us enhance our knowledge in our area of speciality.

Our First Child

Meanwhile, Jaysree was in the family way. It was a matter of happiness for me, but it also meant new responsibilities. I would take her to Kandivali and Mulund, suburbs of Mumbai, for regular medical checkups because the medical facilities were better there. The news also meant that a stream of relatives, from Jashipur and my in-laws' side, began visiting us. My in-laws came to Mumbai for the first time. Jaysree went to Rairangpur when she was eight months pregnant, and our first child, a girl whom we named Debangi, was born there on 28 April 2003. I visited Rairangpur when she was three months old. I cannot describe the happiness I felt holding my sweet little girl in my arms.

Later, after my wife returned to Mumbai with her, we had to quickly readjust our schedules according to our young daughter's needs. She became our topmost priority. Although we had a maid, my wife was busy with household chores. It became difficult for us to even have our dinner in peace; Debangi would insist on disrupting it, and I had to take her in my lap and distract her while I ate. Once, her finger got stuck in the wardrobe door when I shut it, and she was badly hurt. It was a harrowing time for us, but thankfully, with medical attention, the finger healed.

I was back in Kolkata because my seniors decided to bring me back to help our Kolkata unit achieve the Level 3 certification. The summers were terribly hot, and there was no air-conditioner in our house. The power supply was erratic at night, and our daughter would howl loudly when the lights went out. We would fan her with a newspaper or cardboard till she slept.

Once Debangi began to crawl and then walk (we had bought a walker for her), she was always on the lookout to create chaos. I had bought many toys for her to play with, but her attention was always on the books in my room. I was preparing for an examination based on the training I had received in Mumbai. She would creep into my room and pounce on the books to tear the pages, and I would rush to keep them away from her reach. Eventually, I would close the doors of the room when I studied.

When the results were declared, I was among the top five HCL employees who took the test. The certification was important because it was mandatory for employment in the US, and I had the aim to work there. My success encouraged other employees of the company to take the examination.

By the time I returned to Kolkata, a new shopping mall had come up in Salt Lake, called City Centre. I would buy things for Debangi from there and the cities I visited during my business trips. We held a small event called *Anna Prasanna* when she switched from baby food to normal food.

Learning SAP

I was happy on the personal and professional front. At this time, a new business solution in the IT industry, called SAP, began to grab everyone's attention. The name originated from German, Systemanalyse Programmentwicklung, which means system analysis programme development. Put simply, it is an enterprise resource planning (ERP) tool that streamlines and centralizes data management. Traditional business models often de-centralize data management, with each business unit storing its operational data in a separate database. Employees from different business functions find it difficult to access each other's information. In addition, the duplication of data across multiple departments increases IT storage costs and the risk of data errors.

SAP had enormous potential, and I was among the people selected by HCL to specialize in the concept. The training was in Noida, after which I worked to implement it in our Kolkata centre. Debasis Ghosh was the head, and he groomed me. A Chennai-based Bengali, he was not only my senior but also a mentor and friend. After lunch, he would take me for a short walk, enquire about my family and discuss the nitty-gritty of SAP. My trainers were Shushank Sinha and Tejaswini Das. They were excellent, and their teachings were crisp and practical. It was an enormous learning experience for me, and I quickly realized I had to specialize in SAP for my future career prospects.

Incidentally, SAP had been part of my MBA course, but it was purely theoretical. At the end of my training in Noida, my seniors were amazed that I had picked up so much in such a short time, not knowing that I had been initiated into the subject during my MBA days.

The six months after I completed my ERP training were hectic. I regularly visited the North-East, Mumbai and Dhaka on business trips. Sometime in September–October 2004, I moved to Noida with my family for project training. Shakti Guha was our programme manager. We were not used to the bitter cold. We stayed at a guest house and would request hot water, which was brought in buckets. It would then be mixed with room-temperature water; thus, we managed during the winter season. We celebrated the new year by travelling to Jaipur by road with a few friends and their families. From January to March 2005, I was sent to Bangalore as the head of a technical project related to SAP and warehouse management systems of Manhattan Associates. I stayed at upmarket Koramangala. The International Tech Park, commonly called ITPL or ITPB, is a tech park located in Whitefield, Bangalore, which was our workplace, and we would go to the office in the afternoon. Our customer-side lead manager was Lydia (from the US).

Looking back, I can say that those months were hectic and rewarding professionally and personally. Our daughter was growing up, and my professional profile was also being enhanced by the day.

It was time for bigger things.

6
Looking East

I was back in Kolkata by the end of March 2005, after having grasped SAP and successfully implementing it for clients. I got busy training other members of the Kolkata team. At this time, I discovered a new opening in Japan for a SAP Logistics Leader. The Japanese arm of Novartis was an HCL customer. A Swiss multinational corporation based in Basel, Novartis had been consistently ranked among the global giants in the pharmaceutical industry; as recently as in 2022, it was the fourth largest in terms of global revenue.

HCL had an ongoing project with Novartis Japan for SAP implementation. Most of the team was in India, and a small group was in Tokyo. Generally, for such projects, the host country, in this case, Japan, has a smaller number of employees because the major part of the work is contracted to outside parties in India for various business reasons, including the fact that it is more cost-effective.

Unfortunately, some issues had cropped up, and the client was dissatisfied with the progress. One day in April, my senior and mentor, Debasis da, called me and asked me to take charge of the assignment. I was then looking forward to working either in the US or the UK and had been in talks with HCL's senior management team about it. I believed that with my expertise in SAP and the opportunities it offered in the US and UK markets, the move would be good for me.

Therefore, I was reluctant to accept the Japan project. Debasis da assured me that it would be a short stint—no more than three months—and that once the issues were satisfactorily resolved, I could return. I reluctantly agreed. My business visa came through in 10 days, and I boarded a flight to Singapore; after a short transit halt there, I took the next flight and landed in Tokyo at the Narita International Airport. I missed being with my daughter on her birthday that year, which fell a few days after I left.

Before I left, I had taken care to understand a little about the Japanese way of life and business. Through acquaintances, I contacted an elderly Bengali lady who lived close to our Salt Lake home to give me a crash course. She had earlier lived and taught in Japan and was conversant with the country and its people. From her, I learned the basics of Japanese culture and traditions. For instance, I learned that the Japanese emphasize politeness and humility; they consider it improper to challenge superiors or speak in loud tones in the office; they value punctuality; etc. I also picked up a few basic Japanese words and sentences to make myself understood in the initial days. Even after these preparations, I was understandably nervous. I consoled myself with the thought that some colleagues from Kolkata, such as Jitendra Sethi and Bhabani Sahoo, both from Odisha, were already in Tokyo.

I landed in Japan just three or four days before the Golden Week, a seven-day holiday. Every business establishment, including banks, was shut on account of multiple national holidays falling in sequence. The first problem I faced on landing at the airport was currency exchange. I only had dollars, and the currency exchange counters were shut. Because Novartis officials knew of my arrival, the company's chief financial officer, Kobayashi-san, was kind enough to speak with a leading hotel, and the hotel agreed to exchange my US dollars for Japanese yen. I took a bus from the airport and reached the hotel; it was Hotel Villa Fontaine in the Okachimachi area. I was under no illusion that it would be a grand hotel or that the rooms would be spacious, but the room I got was even smaller than I had imagined. Nevertheless, it contained all the basic amenities, and the company paid for my stay there for the initial 5–6 days.

A few days later, I shifted to a furnished accommodation in Crystal Village, Nakano-ku. My workplace was in the World Trade Centre in Tokyo. Our offices were on the 37th floor, from where I had a grand view of the sea, other tall buildings and the city landscape. The office was in Daimon/Hamamatsucho. I had never worked in such a tall building, and it was both scary and exciting. Once, there was a minor earthquake, and because we were on such a high floor, we could really feel the tremor. I was alarmed because it was my first time experiencing an earthquake. I initially travelled to work by the Metro Oedo line and later by the JR line.

Over time, I made several local friends in Japan. I was also able to develop a good rapport with key members of Novartis and win their confidence with my work. They realized I was on the right track and did not escalate any more issues with the higher authorities of HCL in India. Several issues were resolved in the process. That said, I was looking forward to ending my sojourn in Japan by the end of May.

Most of the issues that had caused problems were technical, though the client had categorized them as 'communication'. There were larger issues with project management. I was working on them while developing a close relationship with key stakeholders. The senior executive at Konica Minolta was a tough and uncompromising man, a leader many feared. Everybody wondered how I would deal with him. I was polite and courteous and was accompanied by a technical man in my meetings and even a translator initially. I was told by somebody that he was keen to learn English. I seized the opportunity and boldly made an offer to him: I could teach him English if he could hone my Japanese skills. He sportingly agreed. The arrangement meant that I had easy access to him. Soon, we got along like a house on fire.

As I mentioned, getting the Konica Minolta SAP project contract was not easy. After we worked on a process, we would rehearse it by simulating conditions that tested the system. Errors that came up were rectified. We had as many as three rehearsals during the December year-end holidays before we decided to go live, which meant that the client could use the new SAP from the new year. Despite all the precautions and rehearsals, some problems cropped up, and my team and I, along with Konica Minolta, worked through the day and late into the evenings to fix them. Finally, we put an effective process in place. It was a great achievement, and word about me soon spread in Japan's IT circles. I became a celebrity of sorts! As a result of these achievements, by 2007, HCL began attracting decent quantities of enterprise IT/SAP projects in Japan.

I must emphasize that having a good equation with your client is the key to success. My success would also be good for the senior staff members of the client company because they, too, would be seen as excellent performers. Often, at the end of a day's work, I would present a report and informally discuss matters with senior members of Novartis. This made them happy and satisfied (with my team's work).

Such were my relations with my Japanese clients that they would often take me out for lunch. In contrast, many of my HCL colleagues brought their tiffin boxes because the cost of eating out was prohibitive. I was there for a short duration—or so I had believed—so I had not developed that habit. Over time, my Japanese colleagues even came to know the days of the week I was a vegetarian. If that took care of my lunch, there was still breakfast and dinner to be handled. For breakfast, I managed with bread, butter or cheese and fruits. I can barely cook but somehow managed to cook rice, dal and bitter gourd for dinner.

I had thought of returning to Kolkata after two months, but Novartis and HCL had other ideas. With the global team giving positive feedback about our team's performance, my tenure was extended by another three months, much to my dismay. Now I had to extend the contract for my house and be without my family for some more time. The first was done, but the second was a problem because I was facing issues regarding food, among other things. Meanwhile, HCL bagged more contracts in Japan, and I was told to stay there longer and head a larger team working on SAP. After staying away from my family for 2 months, I put in a request for them to join me. The company accepted the request and agreed to pay for their travel. I also applied for a work visa because I could no longer work on short-term business visa.

Shifting my family from Kolkata to Tokyo posed some problems. My daughter had been admitted to a play school in Salt Lake, and I had already shelled out ₹10,000 as a deposit fee. Getting admission to the play school had not been easy; I had to book a spot months in advance. We did not cancel our daughter's admission because we thought we would return soon and that regaining admission for her would be difficult. Moreover, because it would be my wife's first trip abroad, she was unsure if she could manage on her own. In those days, the immigration staff at Kolkata airport caused lots of problems for travellers, especially those who were first-timers and did not know their way.

Fortunately, the family of one of our colleagues, Bhabani Sahoo, was also joining him in Tokyo. Bhabani was not only a friend but also my right-hand man, always ready to help whenever the need arose. Our families travelled together to Tokyo via Singapore, and I was finally reunited with my wife and daughter. Bhabani worked with me directly and indirectly when I was at HCL until 2013, and he was a great support during those years. We were in regular touch, and he was supposed to work with me in my new venture as he had moved back to Kolkata. Unfortunately, Bhabani is no more. He passed away during the COVID-19 pandemic. I am still in touch with his wife Pinky and their two sons.

My wife was shocked to see the house, even though it was fully furnished, because it was small. There was an attic where one could sleep in case guests came for an overnight stay.

Meanwhile, the Kolkata rental flat I had retained had to be vacated because the landlord wanted it for some of his family members. I began looking for a bigger house. I knew I would have to pay a hefty rent for it, even though I would not immediately start living there.

Time went by, and I was given hints that my stay would be extended further due to HCL receiving more contracts in Japan. I was determined to decline any extension and decided to make the most of my remaining months in the wonderful country. My family, along with those of other Novartis employees, had the thrill of seeing the famous fireworks in the Bay area from our office on the 37th floor of the World Trade Centre in August 2005. Novartis organized food and drinks.

We also visited several interesting places in the city, such as Odaiba Seaside Park; Hakone, where we were mesmerized by five lakes; and Mount Fuji. Our friend circle had grown, and we hosted 'curry parties' for my Japanese friends at our home, where the guests enjoyed Indian curry preparations. One other memorable sight was that of cherry blossoms (or sakura). It was great to witness the colourful spectacle in Tokyo's streets. In March–April 2006, I enjoyed the view with my family, who were seeing it for the first time. We went to Kudanshita in the Nakano area and had a good time.

We moved from the small house we had rented to a family accommodation in Nakano-ku after three months of my family joining me in the city. It was under the Iijima san Crystal village and was expensive. I used to spend 25–30 per cent of my salary on rent alone. Meanwhile, the family was missing Indian entertainment, and we were feeling cut off from the country. We subscribed to the online Indian TV content and watched the programmes on our laptops.

We also attended Durga Puja organized by the Bengali community in the city and loved the Odissi classical dance events; the dances were performed by Japanese girls. Because Indian television channels were not available on cable TV, we rented Hindi film cassettes from a nearby store and watched them at home.

One incident caused us minor discomfort. My wife visited a library in Tokyo with an Indian friend. When she returned home, she realized that her handbag was not with her. It contained the keys to the house, some money and the keys to our Kolkata house. It was late in the evening, and we could not contact the landlord for a duplicate key. We had to spend the night at a friend's place. The following day, we collected the spare key and entered our home. Meanwhile, we contacted the local police. After two or three days, the police informed us that the handbag had been recovered from the library. It was returned to us. All our personal belongings, barring a few yens, were in the bag.

In December 2005, I visited India with my family on a holiday. It was a company-sponsored trip, thanks to Debasis da. My mentor made an exception for me. Because it was a company-paid visit, we had to first land in Kolkata. On our way to Kolkata, we had a two-day halt in Singapore, where we roamed as tourists and made some purchases. From Kolkata, we went to Odisha, and after a welcome break from work and a trip to my wife's native place, Rairangpur, as well as Jashipur, we returned to Tokyo.

I now faced the prospect of an extended stay. I thought I could pursue my career in Japan and look for a long-term career. Although it meant staying away from my family, they supported my decision. My wife accepted the situation and eventually adjusted to the new environment. Slowly, Japanese projects came into my fold, and I began earnestly taking Japanese lessons from a person living close by; my very basic skills in the language would no longer suffice. In fact, I even cleared the Level 4 Japanese Language Proficiency Test (JLPT), which was of a basic level. In reality, I no longer minded the stay. I had got used to Japan's lifestyle and way of work. I loved the Japanese culture and customs. Even so, I believed I would return after a year or two. The thought of going to the US was still at the back of my mind.

Work was proceeding smoothly. Profit margins had increased by nearly twice the previous figures, and I was being recognized for my work. I was regularly invited to leadership meetings hosted by HCL Tech in Japan and India and even won a few awards for my performance. I was fortunate to receive stock options at HCL, a benefit otherwise available only to senior management. I must add here that my domain knowledge in manufacturing and supply chain management, taught to me by Prof. D. Acharya, was very helpful in providing solutions and consulting services to clients.

HCL then suggested I launch a SAP Implementation Services business for the company in Japan so that we could tap other clients as well. SAP was still a new concept in Japan, and there was demand for it. Besides, we had gained considerable exposure and specialization in that domain. I was told that I would head the SAP practice. It was a good opportunity, and I grabbed it with both hands, thinking there was no harm in trying it for two years or so. My juniors, working on projects in Tokyo, had been well-trained by then and could manage on their own.

We got three big contracts, which the new department under me took up. One was for hi-tech maker Konica Minolta, the second for Cadbury, and the third for advertising giant Dentsu. For the Konica Minolta contract, I attended as many as 40 meetings, explaining the process and our proposal in English and Japanese, before it was accepted. It was a technical project. You need patience and technical know-how to close any deal in Japan. It was a major contract; 20 per cent of our revenue came from just this one client. Now I was not only a technical man specializing in SAP but also a business leader attending to issues of profit margins and more. We moved to a bigger office space in 2007 and partnered with a Japanese consulting firm to get more clients. Our customer base continued growing. We added another major client: Merck. The decision to start a separate SAP business yielded good results in Japan.

My desire to continuously upgrade my knowledge led me

to complete a certification course in SAP Order Fulfilment/ SD from Japan. I became a certified project management professional (PMP) in 2003 and needed to get it renewed every three years with the professional development unit. This, like the SAP certification, had great value in Japan, and I was encouraged to mention the achievement on my business cards. I also did a SAP Materials Management/ Procurement certification course, thus improving my holistic understanding of the corporate sector—a quality that was much admired in Japan.

On the personal front, I got Debangi admitted to a kindergarten school, the Global Indian International School (GIIS) in Mizue, Tokyo. Although the school was good, it was more than one hour by train from our home in Nakano. This meant that my daughter (and my wife who dropped her to school and picked her up) had to spend two hours travelling every day. It began impacting their health; my little daughter would experience bouts of vomiting. A month after admitting her there, we moved close to the school to Mizue, Edogawa-ku, Tokyo. Incidentally, HCL had moved its offices to a more spacious premise in Kudanshita, which was half an hour by train from our new residence. Also, the Indian embassy in Tokyo was within walking distance from this place.

Getting the accommodation was not easy. I could not rent a private apartment without the company leasing and paying for it or without a guarantor. I spoke with the HCL management, but the company did not have a policy of leasing out homes for its staff. A solution was eventually found, and I suspect this was because the management realized my criticality to the ongoing projects and my bright track record. The company agreed to lease the accommodation and pay the rent directly to the landlord after deducting the amount from my salary. Debangi studied there for five years. It was a good location. There were sports facilities like tennis courts, swimming pool and parks. It was where I started learning to play tennis and practising my swimming skills. Playing tennis was another dream come true because earlier, I could not indulge in this hobby as it is an expensive game and finding a tennis court was a challenge. Debangi started learning to swim at a nearby swimming club. She also began to play soft tennis here.

Meanwhile, a senior HCL executive and president of the Japan unit, Arasu-san, came to know about my contribution and heartily applauded my work. I was to get recognition at the country-level award ceremony for my contribution to customer satisfaction and new business development. I also managed to build a good team over time. Recognition was not new to me; in 2006, HCL awarded me a customer satisfaction award personally signed by our promoter, Shiv Nadar.

In 2007, we threw a big birthday party for Debangi, wherein we invited my colleagues and friends from the office, my daughter's school friends and my wife's acquaintances and friends. We ordered food and had a merry time. Another major event occurred on the personal front. In 2007, my elder brother's daughter got married, for which I spent a considerable amount of money. After all, they were family, and I had not forgotten the help my brother had extended to me during my school and college days. We also made an investment decision, purchasing a flat in Kolkata from a Singapore-based real estate owner. We still have it. I wanted to sell it later, but my wife decided we should keep it. The flat is in the Rajarhat area called Elita Garden Vista.

Little did I know my decision to stay back in Japan would become a turning point in my life and career.

7
Expansion and Consolidation

The period from 2007 to 2008 was one of expansion and consolidation for HCL's SAP and Enterprise IT business in Japan. We succeeded because of the effectiveness of the solutions we devised and our approach towards business in general. I realized our Japanese clients were not impressed by verbosity but by to-the-point presentations and solutions to possible challenges related to execution. Thus, I ensured that whenever my team made a pitch, they gave precise and direct presentations, cutting out the flab. I have mentioned my efforts to learn Japanese. The desire was driven by the acknowledgement that proficiency in the local language would help me communicate with clients and make a good impression, which would help us secure more business and sustain it.

I noted that although several Japanese firms were multinational, very few of their top executives could communicate in English, which was a global language. This was an opportunity for us. On the one hand, we were learning to communicate with them in Japanese. On the other hand, we helped firms with a global presence with our English language skills.

Kiyoshi Takigawa san was the general manager and SAP head of Konica Minolta Information Systems, one of our biggest clients. He would encourage me to speak in Japanese during the meetings, but his English was weak. Because we got along well, he asked me to help him with his English, and I agreed. Conversely, I requested him to help me improve my Japanese, and he graciously accepted. It took me a year and a half to clear the Japanese Level 3 exams, and after that, I could converse in the local language quite effectively.

Takigawa-san was a powerful executive and well-known not only in his company but also in Japan's corporate sector for his no-nonsense approach. He led a team of almost 200 people. When we had pitched for the Konica Minolta business, I would travel three to four days a week to the client's office, which was in Tachikawa, a 90-minute journey by train from my residence.

Meanwhile, we managed to develop really good content for our business and a differentiator in the Japanese market in the enterprise/SAP business. Yoichi Tomioka, my colleague who was working with our partner at Zacatii Consulting, played a critical role in our expansion. Occasionally, he would also help me with the local language. Although he was not a SAP/ERP expert, he was young, dynamic and willing to learn. He helped us develop an effective sales kit, which our people back home had been unable to do. Looking back, I now understand that our earlier solution models had failed in Japan because our approach was different, and we were unable to understand their specific requirements. This was because of our poor language skills and a lack of understanding of Japan's business culture.

How I Became Mr SAP

It was around the end of 2007 that HCL Chief Shiv Nadar visited Tokyo. By then, our SAP business was doing quite well and held promise for further expansion. However, HCL's core interest was still in research and development (R&D) and conventional software development, and it had a major presence in these areas in Japan. HCL's senior management back in India did not consider the SAP business as a major portfolio for the company despite its growth. Although I never got to meet Nadar one-on-one, I attended a meeting he conducted during his Japan visit. There were around 300 people, including executives from Japan. India's ambassador to Japan, Hemant Krishan Singh, had also been invited. Nadar thought big; everything he did and wanted to do was on a big scale. He was ambitious and focused. After the meeting, all of us sat down with drinks, and he was more relaxed and spoke with us informally.

HCL's focus on conventional business was because that was what its senior management believed in. Nevertheless, my SAP team continued to do well, even if it was not getting the recognition it deserved. It was only after Vineet Nayar, whom I mentioned earlier, took charge that HCL's top management gave our SAP business the attention it deserved. Nayar recognized that SAP could be one of HCL's major portfolios. Over time, we landed Nippon Telegraph and Telephone (NTT) and Nippon Electric Company (NEC) (the Nippon Group is a Japanese multinational information technology and electronics corporation) as our clients. We successfully completed several projects by the end of December and I was personally present for the trials and rollout of the product we had developed.

Here, I must give credit to the members of the excellent onsite team: Bhabani Sahoo, Paritosh Manna, Ritesh Shrivastav, etc. In India, Nikilesh Dey and Sulagna Dasgupta were pillars of strength. The project went live in the first week of January 2008, and even though we had niggling issues, we successfully resolved them. The model was appreciated at different forums in Japan and across HCL in the SAP business unit. It was the first such execution of a large project. Based on this success, we received other projects from the same client for global rollouts.

I was lucky to get encouragement from my seniors at HCL. The SAP Practice Head Murali Raghavan was like a mentor to me. HCL Japan President S.T. Arasu also backed me fully. Top leaders like Prem Kumar and J. Kalyan Raman kept visiting Japan to fine-tune our sales strategy and support my efforts. I fondly remember listening to and receiving guidance from Prem Kumar. Soon, I came to be known as Mr SAP.

My desire to learn more never dimmed. I got various SAP certifications like SAP Procurement and Solution Manager. Around that time, our visionary CEO began programmes like the HCL Scholar certification, which was a must for all customer-facing senior executives, including the president of HCL Japan. It helped us know HCL's capabilities in detail and share the know-how with one another.

I wanted to share my knowledge on project management, so I took a lead role in the HCL Project Management Council in Japan. I was elected to this position through on-site voting by employees. HCL human resources leader Kamal Chauhan and my colleague Issac Newton backed me. We were considered employee-first leaders; the HCL chief had a new policy of 'employee first; customer second'. A book was published on the subject, which is available in the market. On the weekends, we used to conduct project management council meetings in the office, and many participants, usually manager-level, shared their knowledge. We also helped new members prepare for the PMP exam. We used to invite different leaders to speak to the participants. Many participants today hold good positions in Japan and outside.

HCL had, over time, established a 360-degree feedback test. It was mandatory for manager-level personnel to clear that test. Incidentally, I was among the top five scorers in this category across different locations outside India. In Japan, I continued to score the highest. This greatly motivated my colleagues and I. Sometime in 2008, HCL Japan President Arasu retired and Hari Bhat succeeded him. I developed a good rapport with him, and we still maintain a close relationship to this day.

While my career was proceeding smoothly, I was involved in some personal matters that were a source of satisfaction and happiness for me. As I mentioned earlier, we had moved close to Global Indian International School. The school attracted several Indian families, who had also shifted base nearby for the sake of their children. Consequently, I became acquainted with many Indian families, some of whom were from Odisha. We met occasionally and became friends. A few families from Odisha floated the idea of conducting a Saraswati Puja. Partha Mishra, Sarat Sahoo, Tathagata Sahoo and Sudhir Mishra were among them. We organized the event successfully. We then decided to organize a Jagannath Rath Yatra in June 2008. The event would be the first of its kind in Japan, and we had to get permission from the local authorities to hold the event in Saitama-Misato, a town adjacent to Tokyo. We presented the event as a cultural and not religious function because the latter categorization could have led the authorities to reject our request. Once we got the go-ahead, preparations began in full swing. A core team of 10–12 members was formed to oversee the execution of the arrangements.

Many issues had to be taken care of: funds collection, getting sponsorships, the construction of the chariot, arranging for food, holding cultural shows, etc. Because we were organizing the event for the first time, we had no experience and struggled a lot. However, we were determined, and despite the challenges, we managed to organize everything. We received support from not only the Indian community but also locals such as Yano. It was such a happy moment when we pulled the chariot of Lord Jagannath, Balabhadra and Subhadra. Encouraged by the success, we held the event again in 2009 on a grander scale. It was a matter of pride for Jaysree and me that Debangi performed a dance on the occasion. I believe that the successful organization of the event strengthened the bonds among the Indian diaspora in Japan.

The Indian diaspora was rather small in those days, but today, the Indian community is notably large and influential in many parts of the world. They are also better organized. Over the last few years, especially since Narendra Modi became Prime Minister, the Indian diaspora has gained strength, and the Prime Minister's engagement with them when he travels overseas has added to their influence. In fact, the diaspora plays a big role in organizing such outreach. There is also a better connection between the Indian diaspora and Indian embassies and high commissioners abroad.

Spreading Wings

As HCL's SAP business became firmly rooted in and around Tokyo, we decided to expand elsewhere in Japan. Until now, we were concentrating on Greater Tokyo—Kawasaki, Yokohama, Saitama and Tokyo—and did well for ourselves. In 2008, our senior management back home believed we had to explore more business opportunities and spread our wings in other regions of Japan. I also believed in that idea, having studied the emerging and potential markets outside greater Tokyo.

Therefore, I began undertaking frequent trips out of Greater Tokyo. I travelled to Nagoya, one of the three major cities besides Tokyo and Osaka. It is an industrial and technological city and is best known as an automotive hub, with brands such as Toyota and Denso headquartered there. Mitsubishi Motors has its R&D unit in the city's suburbs, and major component suppliers, such as PPG and Magna Component Suppliers, also have a strong presence.

I also visited Kyoto, some 400 km from Tokyo. A former capital of Japan, it is not an industrial hub, but traditional R&D facilities and intellectual property (IP)-based companies have a big presence there. It is also home to Horiba Ltd. Horiba manufactures instruments that measure and analyse automobile exhaust gas and environmental, medical and scientific applications. The firm is one of the world's top 25 analytical and life sciences instrumentation companies.[2]

I also made trips to Osaka, Japan's second-biggest city. It is a prominent industrial base, with companies such as Bridgestone located there, and is around 500 km from Tokyo. Another place I regularly visited was Hamamatsucho, where automotive firms Suzuki and Yamaha are located. Yamaha is strong in the automotive sector and musical instruments business. We pursued Enterprise transformation opportunities in Yamaha for their musical instruments segment. I also visited Fukuoka, 750 km from Tokyo. It has been an international commercial destination since ancient times. Today, it is home to several notable commercial organizations such as Yaskawa Electric Corporation, which manufactures servos, motion controllers, industrial robots, etc.

Without bullet train services, it would have been difficult

---

[2]Thayer, Ann M., 'Top Instrument Firms', *Chemical & Engineering News*, Vol. 89, 2011, No. 17, 13–19, https://tinyurl.com/3t9k7eh3. Accessed on 23 February 2025.

for me to regularly travel between these far-flung cities and Tokyo. In fact, those trips were fun because travel via bullet trains is smooth and you can work while travelling. I would use the fastest bullet train service, called Nozomi, to reach some of the destinations. The trip between Tokyo and Osaka, for instance, takes just a little under two and a half hours, but because the train did not halt at all the destinations I had to visit, I also used the two other bullet train services, Hikari and Kodama, which had stops there. I would make one or two trips every week to make sales pitches and, after their success, to discuss the global implementation and rollout of the services for our newly acquired clients in those cities. I was a hands-on manager. It was not easy to get those businesses, and I had multiple meetings with the clients to develop trust and demonstrate our execution capabilities. Here, our track record with major firms such as Konica Minolta helped us enormously.

Seizing Opportunities

In those days, Satyam Computer Systems was very successful. Satyam had a wonderful team of people who took the company forward. However, the company faced a major crisis in early 2009 when the company's founder-chairman, Ramalinga Raju, admitted to inflating the company's assets by one billion dollars. This led to criminal charges and a collapse in the company's stock price. Eventually, Mahindra Group's IT arm, Tech Mahindra, purchased a major stake in the company. In 2009, the company was renamed Mahindra Satyam. Mahindra Satyam merged with Tech Mahindra in 2013.[3]

---

[3]Bhasin, Madan Lal, 'Creative Accounting Scam at Satyam Computer Limited: How the Fraud Story Unfolded?', *Open Journal of Accounting*,

Satyam's collapse sent shockwaves across the Indian corporate sector, especially the IT industry, but it was a blessing in disguise for us. Nayar, our visionary and aggressive leader, began globally seeking out Satyam's brightest employees who faced an uncertain future. We went on overdrive and began hiring the best minds from the sinking company. In Nagoya, for instance, where we had an ongoing project, we picked up Satyam's team of 15 personnel. We hit two birds with one stone. One, we got good people to join our team, and two, we added new customers because the clients the Satyam team was working with also came to us. Thus, overnight, our team of experts grew, as did our customer base.

Meanwhile, I had another opportunity to enhance our business profile. The Japan SAP Users Group (JSUG) was (and still is) an influential gathering of senior personnel involved in the SAP business, and they are drawn from various reputed Japanese companies. They would meet and discuss various issues related to SAP and ERP, point out problems and suggest solutions. I was introduced to JSUG by some senior employees at Konica Minolta and became a member. It was a prestigious matter for me to be part of this group. It held two advantages. One, I gained access to important people in decision-making positions in different Japanese companies, which later helped me expand HCL's client base. Two, it provided us with an opening to interact with SAP headquarters in Germany. Several tricky issues that our people could not resolve because of complications would be referred to SAP Germany, and we would receive the necessary assistance. This helped us provide effective and timely solutions to our clients. HCL partnered with JSUG, and we were soon giving joint presentations to potential clients.

A Major Acquisition

HCL made a valuable acquisition that enhanced its global presence and profile. In December 2008, HCL Technologies announced that it had closed a deal to acquire UK-based SAP consulting company AXON Group Plc.[4] It said that the merger presented a great opportunity to bring new capabilities to the market with a global delivery system model. It promised to provide the full life cycle suite of services that fit HCL's new growth strategy. CEO Nayar stated that HCL had extensive experience in ensuring smooth integration and preserving the unique identity and character of the companies it acquired.

Talks had been ongoing for several months for the acquisition. Nayar believed that the acquisition would help us tackle the chinks in our SAP armour. I was also involved in the management discussions. Although we were good at SAP, when it came to the full package—Oracle, Microsoft and SAP—we had limitations. Firms such as Accenture and Satyam were ahead of us. AXON had the domain knowledge we lacked, and it had a footprint across the world that we did not. Its SAP business was five times that of ours. Nevertheless, we had one advantage it did not: we were strong in Japan, and AXON had virtually no presence in that market. So the merger was also beneficial to it. However, HCL was not alone in wanting to acquire it; Infosys was also in the fray, but fortunately for HCL, it did not move fast enough.

---

[4]'HCL Tech Completes Axon Acquisition', *Business Standard*, 20 January 2013, https://tinyurl.com/mv5kz34j. Accessed on 23 February 2025.

Most of AXON's top management was from the UK, while some of them were from Australia; very few came from Asia. One outcome of the merger was that I was appointed the North Asia Head of HCL–AXON and reported directly to the Asia Pacific Japan Head, Brian Pereira, who was based in Australia. During the initial five years, my reporting head kept changing. It would be Richard Gu (Shanghai), Ruth Rudwick (Malaysia) and Bala Nair (Malaysia). HCL Japan Chief Hari Bhat remained a pillar of strength for me, and although I did not report to him, I closely interacted with him. His wife, a Japanese national, was an Odissi dancer. Similarly, Sivaram Dhara, a senior HCL Japan executive, though not in my reporting line, was always there when I needed advice. He taught me the virtues of patience and to think before acting. Sunil Viswanathan, another senior executive of HCL Japan, remains a close friend of mine to this day. He gave me valuable lessons in branding. I had the opportunity to interact with another remarkable person, Virendra Agrawal. Based in Singapore, he taught me the art of closing deals effectively and quickly. I recall Anand Murali. Although he was not part of HCL–AXON, he shared some of my work, and because there was mutual understanding and respect, we complemented each other.

Earlier, I was an Indian employee deputed to Japan, and my salary had two components: one from India and another from Japan. After becoming a part of HCL–AXON, I was considered an HCL employee from Japan, so the Indian component of the salary was discontinued. It became difficult for me to maintain a decent lifestyle with the revised amount. My market value had increased, but at HCL, recognition comes step by step. Fortunately, HCL–AXON had an employee-friendly policy, and I received an additional 20 per cent over and above my salary, which was of great help.

After the reverse merger[5] of HCL Technologies with AXON, there was some turmoil within the company because it made certain staff redundant. When two firms merge, it results in surplus staff, especially at the top level. You cannot have two CEOs, two CFOs, two delivery heads, and so on. Many senior HCL employees, facing instability, quit the company. I wasn't affected because I was in charge of SAP operations in Japan and virtually managing the business independently. It would not have been easy to replace me. Besides, I had excellent relations with the company's seniors back in India, and they recognized my contribution. I received good salary hikes (almost 25–30 per cent, while the average annual increase in Japan was not more than 5 per cent) and got promoted to associate general manager, even as I continued to head the North Asia market. I had every reason to feel satisfied.

One of the largest deals I was involved in during those days was to bring GSK, a major pharmaceutical company, as a client. One-third of HCL's global ERP revenues would later come from this one client. GSK had a strong presence in Japan, so I was involved in winning the deal. My experience with the Novartis SAP projects, on which I had worked from scratch, and my knowledge of taxation, legal and statutory aspects helped us bag the client. My team made presentations in London, and the GSK top brass was impressed. I met AXON Chief Steve Cardell. Chris Murrey, a senior executive, became a good friend. It took over three years for the GSK rollout to be done in Japan.

---

[5]The HCL Enterprise business was carved out and merged with AXON and the new entity HCL AXON was run by AXON.

Despite my performance, I had to fight for sales credit for my region—Japan—so that it showed up in my portfolio. I told Steve it was only fair that at least the part of the sales we secured was shown in my portfolio because I played a critical role in getting the business. He agreed.

With the creation of HCL–AXON and my promotion to North Asia Head, things became even more hectic for me. Besides discharging my responsibilities, I had to make business trips to Europe (Holland, Belgium and France) in 2008 along with the tech lead and team member Pankaj Goel. I used the occasion to take my family along on some of those visits. In Holland, we had a wonderful Tulip Experience at the Keukenhof. We also saw the Eiffel Tower in Paris.

Satisfying Moments

Meanwhile, I continued to upgrade my domain expertise. If one does not keep abreast with changing technology, one runs the risk of losing the competitive edge. I began learning the best practices of transition methodology or IT Infrastructure Library and IT Service Management (ITIL-ITSM). I also regularly travelled to Singapore and India (Noida) for various business-related matters.

On the personal front, apart from the occasional trips outside Japan, my family enjoyed my daughter's birthday celebrations, which we held in Mizue-Edogawa-ku, Tokyo. We invited several friends and acquaintances, and the turnout was large. The guests included members of the Odiya community, which gladdened our hearts. Moreover, for a third year in a row, in 2010, our community organized the Jagannath Rath Yatra, this time on a larger scale in Yamashita Koen in Yokohama. It is an iconic park, and getting permission was not easy. We also held several Indian dance performances, such as Bharatanatyam and Odissi.

The Indian Deputy Chief of Mission—DCM Sanjay Panda—who was from Odisha, was really helpful and encouraging. We received a great amount of guidance. Another event we held yet again was the Saraswati Puja in February 2010, which was on a much bigger scale than the previous year. Here, a prominent Indian (also from Odisha), Dr Sarat Sahoo, was at the forefront in helping me organize the event. He became a friend with whom I am still in touch. He is a scientist and chemical engineer working with the International Atomic Energy Agency.

My family and a few other Indian families (primarily Odias) visited Mount Fuji. We stayed there for two days and had great fun.

All in all, 2009 and 2010 were good for me professionally and personally.

8
The Calamity and After

As part of HCL–AXON, my team and I now had greater exposure to not just SAP but also ERP packages like Oracle and Microsoft. We continued to progress in the Japanese market with the help of our back-office support teams in Kolkata and Noida. I had a team of around 40 people, including Japanese nationals. Some of them were actually paid higher salaries than me. I negotiated the higher pay for them because I realized that one could not get the best people at low salaries. Although the team from India did the actual work, the Japanese people's presence helped us acquire new businesses and increase our revenues. To that extent, the decision to pay them high salaries was justified. That said, I remained a hands-on manager.

From 2010 onwards, we started a development centre that focused on the application support team in Kuala Lumpur, Malaysia. I would frequently travel there to oversee the new operations. There were pros and cons to having the Kuala Lumpur office. One benefit was the time zone; the time difference between Tokyo and Kuala Lumpur was barely an hour (it was three and a half hours between India and Japan, with Japan ahead), thereby making coordination easier and faster. The other benefit was that the back-office team in Kuala Lumpur had more skills and were better qualified than the teams back in India. This helped us provide better products and services to our clients in Japan.

The disadvantage was that barely anyone in our Kuala Lumpur office could speak Japanese, so it became a problem for them to communicate directly with our clients. Furthermore, the cost of maintaining the back office in Kuala Lumpur was higher than in India. Because the amount we received from our clients was the same, regardless of whether we used our Kuala Lumpur or India back office, the Kuala Lumpur operations cut into our profit margins. Overall, however, we gained from the Kuala Lumpur office.

Meanwhile, we also ventured into creating an IT product for maintenance, repair and overhaul (MRO) services for airlines. The product was aimed at ensuring that the aircraft were always ready to fly. Doing so involved a series of software solutions to streamline airline functioning. It was a new line of business for us, and success did not come easy. Eventually, we managed to get a few customers. We made several sales pitches through meetings and seminars at prominent hotels across Japan, where I was a regular speaker. It was a novel experience for me and helped broaden my professional horizon.

Basically, the software product tracked the schedule for the maintenance, repair or replacement of the thousands of parts in an aircraft. The previous manual system was time-consuming and difficult to remember. Schedules were often skipped because somebody failed to remember at the right time. With the MRO product, all one had to do was tap a few keys on the computer to get the entire schedule before one's eyes. In other words, both kinds of MRO—reactive and predictive—were tackled efficiently. Reactive MRO is the action taken when some part develops a sudden fault and must be repaired, whereas predictive MRO keeps track of the short- or long-term repairs or replacements of parts.

The product was also useful for the railway industry, and HCL–AXON tried to get rail services interested. We made several presentations to different customers, but nothing came of it.

The basic product had been created by AXON before it became part of HCL. About 150–200 people had worked on it, but we tweaked it to suit client requirements when we introduced it in Japan. It was already being used by customers in Malaysia, the UAE, Europe, etc.

The Fukushima Disaster

In December 2010, my family and I visited India for a long vacation, returning in early March. Little did we know that in just a few weeks, we would face a disaster of catastrophic proportions. It was around noon on 11 March 2011, and my colleagues and I were in our 10th-floor office in Tokyo, busy as usual with meetings, presentations, etc. Suddenly, the building began shaking perilously. It seemed the structure would crumble at any moment, burying us under debris. We knew it was a major earthquake and rushed to the ground floor, taking the stairs because using the lift was out of the question. There was a mad rush among the people to escape at the earliest. One of our colleagues jumped two or three steps at a time and fell to the ground, fracturing his bone.

I witnessed chaotic scenes outside. The streets were filled with people anxious to escape. All transport systems had come to a halt; neither trains nor buses nor taxis were available. Everyone was walking, mostly to their homes; many would have to trek long distances to reach their destinations.

Before leaving the office, I had managed to contact my family by landline and was relieved to know they were safe. I, too, reconciled myself to a long walk but was lucky to get a bicycle from a colleague. But I could not ride as the roads were crowded with people walking towards their homes. Even before we left the office, at least three more tremors had hit Tokyo.

Information soon began filtering in, and we realized the enormity of the crisis. The earthquake epicentre was 200 km from Tokyo, and yet, the tremors were so severe that the scale of the earthquake had to be high; it was of a magnitude of nine. We would soon learn about the other related disasters. More than 20,000 people lost their lives.

That fateful day, a magnitude 9 undersea mega-thrust earthquake hit the Pacific Ocean a little over 72 km east of Oshika Peninsula in the Tohoku region. It lasted for approximately six minutes and triggered a tsunami. It was the most powerful earthquake ever recorded in Japan (and the fourth most powerful in the world) since 1900 when modern seismological calculations began to be recorded. The tsunami waves were as high as 133 metres in Miyako, and in the Sendai area, the wind travelled at a speed of 700 km/hour; inland, the speed was up to 10 km/hour. The worst was yet to come. The resulting snowfall compounded the tragedy. The temperature in Ishinomaki was 0°C, and there were reports of people dying due to the intense cold.[6]

As if this was not enough, the Fukushima Daiichi nuclear plant was impacted. Three of its reactors went into meltdown, and radioactive substances spread in the city, affecting hundreds of thousands of residents.[7] Electrical

---

[6]'Mar 11, 2011 CE: Tohoku Earthquake and Tsunami', *National Geographic*, https://tinyurl.com/35n6335u. Accessed on 23 February 2025.
[7]'Fukushima Daiichi Accident', *World Nuclear Association*, 29 April 2024,

generators ran out of fuel, and cooling systems shut down, thus allowing heat to build up. This led to the generation of hydrogen gas, and without adequate ventilation, the refuelling hall exploded.

Initial estimates projected the losses due to the earthquake, and it became one of the costliest natural disasters in history. Needless to say, it set back Japan's economic development.[8]

Challenges After the Calamity

The calamity also affected HCL's workforce. Besides the disruptions in daily routines, the fear of radiation loomed large. We were worried for ourselves and our families. Several HCL employees sent requests to be shifted out of Japan. Because senior management did not officially give them permission, they left on their own. HCL–AXON also saw some of its Indian staff leave Japan, but by and large, we were not severely impacted because many of our staff members were from Japan. Meanwhile, I made a quick visit to India to drop my family and returned without my clients noticing my absence.

Our Japanese customers were very upset with the exodus of HCL's staff and considered the 'desertion' a lack of loyalty. Their anger was not directed at HCL alone; other Indian firms had also shifted their staff, with L&T even chartering a flight to evacuate their employees and their families. I tried to convince them otherwise, explaining that the decision had nothing to do with their lack of love for Japan and its people, which remained as high as before. They were only

---

https://tinyurl.com/5n9aby4v. Accessed on 23 February 2025.
[8]Goyette, Pierre, 'The Economic Impacts of the Fukushima Disaster (2025)', *Custommapposter*, 21 February 2025, https://tinyurl.com/67xrj6ny. Accessed on 23 February 2025.

apprehensive about the fallouts of the disaster. I pointed out that much of my team and I were still in Japan and serving our Japanese clients.

Although they were pleased with our commitment, the markets became wary of giving us new business. We must have lost quite a few opportunities to secure contracts. Potential customers were apprehensive that our employees would desert them midway, thus causing delays in execution. Meanwhile, HCL had to issue 'apology letters' to our existing clients for leaving them midstream. Those who left never returned. They wanted to work from home in India, but the company put its foot down. Consequently, they quit and sought employment elsewhere, either in India, the US or Europe.

Taking advantage of the situation, some local vendors who had lost out to us in business began to whisper in the ears of our potential and existing clients that we could not be trusted. They managed to get some of our future businesses. Because they were Japanese vendors, they had the upper hand at that time.

The first year of the disaster was challenging for us. Because several people had quit Japan, we were short on manpower. Servicing existing businesses became an issue, let alone acquiring new ones, though at HCL–AXON, we managed the situation quite well.

Meanwhile, we had taken some precautions at a personal level. We switched over to food products that came from outside Japan. We bought our daily essentials, such as vegetables and other edible products, from stores that stocked goods imported from the US, India, Thailand, Vietnam, etc. We even bought milk and water from these outlets, worried about the effects of radiation from Japanese products. We also stopped shaving and getting haircuts outside, preferring to trim our hair and shave at home. Later, as the threat waned, we switched to Japanese products that came from closer to Tokyo and far away from Fukushima.

I even began studying the effects of radiation on the Internet. I learned that Sievert is a unit of ionizing radiation equal to 100 rems; rem is a dosage unit of X-ray and gamma-ray radiation exposure. Although that extra exposure can increase the risk of cancer, the impact is very small. A 20-milli-sievert-per-year exposure might increase the odds of getting cancer by a few thousandths of a per cent. Needless to say, this information significantly placated my agitated mind.[9]

Meanwhile, we shifted our office from Tokyo to Osaka. The overall situation in those days was confusing, as I repeatedly pointed out to our Japanese customers. The government was not releasing enough information, perhaps worried that such a move would fuel disquiet and chaos. In many cities, there was a shortage of essential items. People were wary of buying vegetables, fearing they might have been contaminated by radiation. Global media was reporting about the tragedy, and Indian media was no exception. However, when I scanned the reports in the Indian press, I was amazed at the factual inaccuracies; they were reporting that Tokyo had been severely hit and the situation was nearly out of control. This was not true. In the initial weeks, things were difficult, but the situation was soon brought under control. My friend, Dr Sarat Sahoo, worked closely with the Japanese government to contain the aftermath of the nuclear disaster.

My family joined me three months later. Soon, it was time for the Rath Yatra celebrations. We held the event in

---

[9]'FAQs', *Japan Atomic Energy Agency*, 11 May 2011, https://tinyurl.com/3s4cxeny. Accessed on 23 February 2025.

a large hall, but the festivities were contained given the recent tragedy. Soon after the calamity, the then Lok Sabha Speaker Meira Kumar and eminent Odissi dancer Sujata Mohapatra visited Japan. I was involved in organizing a part of their visit.

Looking Ahead

A year after the earthquake, things began to get back to normal. Public health experts agreed that radiation fears had been overblown. Compared with the effects of the radiation exposure from Fukushima, 'the number of expected fatalities is never going to be that large,' said Thomas E. McKone of the University of California, Berkeley, School of Public Health.[10] His voice was influential; he would later become Professor Emeritus at the UC Berkeley School of Public Health and advisor to Lawrence Berkeley National Laboratory on sustainable energy systems.

When life was returning to normal, I organized a major SAP marketing event in 2012 at ANA Hotel, a leading hotel in Tokyo. Several bigwigs of the corporate sector attended. The event was prominently reported in the local media, which helped us gain traction and recover. Soon, business began to pick up pace.

I secured a salary hike of nearly 20 per cent and was promoted to deputy general manager. I had also accumulated the stock options due to me in my five years of service. HCL gave stocks in instalments over five years, thus incentivizing senior employees to stay on for at least five years. Despite the hike, my salary was low by Japanese standards. This

---

[10]'Dealing with the Japan Disaster: Earthquake, Tsunami, and Nuclear Risk', *ACOEM International Section* | *International SOS*, 30 June 2011, https://tinyurl.com/yjen9bb6. Accessed on 23 February 2025.

was because I had started at a low salary base, and even after repeated increments, it was not high enough to be considered among the best in Japan for a person of my experience and corporate stature.

The Fukushima disaster led to the exodus of several Indian employees from HCL and other Indian firms based in Japan. Perhaps carried away by that migration, I even began contemplating a shift out of Japan. HCL would never agree to my relocation to India, given I was leading the company to better and better performance in Japan. Therefore, I had to consider switching to another IT company. Another reason why I entertained the thought was my salary. Although it had been enhanced, it was low in comparison with Japan's market rates. My expenses had gone up after I shifted my residence to Setagaya-ku, an upscale locality in Tokyo, in 2012. The rent there was twice what I paid for the earlier house. My decision to shift had to do with Debangi's school. Once her admission was finalized, we moved.

Debangi was now studying at Seisen International School, an elite girls' school. The fee was four times what I paid for her old school. The new school had a tough admission process; there were multiple interviews, and my daughter's academic and extracurricular track records were taken into consideration. She had always been an excellent student, which helped her gain admission. My wife and I did not choose the school because we wanted to boast about privilege or exclusivity but because we wanted to give her the best we could afford.

These developments led me to explore better-paying prospects. I reached out to a friend in the US, and through him, I secured an offer letter from a US firm. Armed with that letter, I applied for an H-1B visa, and my application was approved. I was ready to move out of Japan. However, I had second thoughts. First, I was not certain of my prospects in the US. I would have to start out at a level lower than the one I held in Japan. Second, even if the salary was better, the costs would also be high and neutralize the high salary.

Then I toyed with the idea of relocating to India. I applied to a few leading companies and got a good response. Here, too, I had second thoughts. I would have to look for a suitable school for my daughter; the constant switch could impact her academics. The salaries offered were not to my liking. Moreover, the offers I received were in Bengaluru. I would have to set up things from scratch there. Had I got suitable offers in Kolkata, I might have considered them favourably because I had lived there and was familiar with the city. However, Kolkata had limited senior-level openings of the kind I wanted.

Eventually, I gave up the idea of moving and remained in Tokyo for the time being.

9

Moving Ahead and Moving On

Business continued to grow in 2012–2013. I had completed more than a decade at HCL and was at the peak of my career. My experience was more of an enterprise IT business, wherein I was in charge of my team. I had every reason to feel good because I had started from scratch. Around that time, there was some reshuffling in the top hierarchy of HCL Technologies in Japan and Asia Pacific. A few senior members from the Asia Pacific Japan Singapore division, whom I knew well and had developed a sound working relationship with—I did not report to them but had to collaborate with them on some accounts—quit the company. Because they were not directly connected with my portfolio, this development had a limited impact on my business.

Later, several people from our Kolkata development centre, with whom I had developed a good rapport, also left. After that, I reduced my dependence on the Kolkata office and routed most of my work through the offices in Noida, Kuala Lumpur and Singapore, where we had opened a small unit.

A Major Agreement

At the end of 2012 and the beginning of 2013, we cracked a major deal, which was the first such agreement, between HCL Japan and the D+M Group, known worldwide for its high-quality consumer audio products. D+M's brands included Denon and Marantz. The deal was considered a 'transformational agreement'—which would help reconfigure the implementation of financial services from SAP and other related applications—for the company's Japan operations. It would also help align the company's code structure.

The agreement was based on a global delivery model, through which HCL Japan would support D+M entities in Japan, the US, China and Europe. By now, HCL has had over 17 years of experience with SAP and more than 6,000 consultants across 31 countries. Following the new arrangement, D+M expected that its closing activities, which, at that time, required substantial manual interventions related to accounts receivable and payable activities, would be simplified with the implementation of SAP solutions. HCL would also address issues such as a lack of organized tools for capital budgeting and cash flow forecasting.

Our Enterprise Application Services (EAS) division's global capability was a big differentiator in helping us seize the transformational deal. D+M Group had approximately 2,000 employees worldwide, with products and services sold in over 45 countries. It was a Bain Capital portfolio company. The EAS division was a business transformation consultancy that delivered significant value to large, complex organizations through the innovative implementation and support of enterprise applications.

The day the deal was announced, HCL's share price shot up by 1 per cent. It was a memorable day for me, as the impact was felt across HCL.

Addressing the Gartner Conference

I believe the opportunity to speak at the prestigious annual Gartner Conference was among the most memorable moments of my career. Gartner Inc. is a US-based agency that provides cutting-edge guidance to the IT industry and rates IT companies based on a host of parameters. These ratings are highly valued in the IT sector. A high rating instantly places a company in the big league and helps it acquire a positive profile and new businesses. Based in Stanford, it conducts research on technology and shares the outcomes through private consulting as well as executive programmes and conferences.

Gartner provides opportunities for senior IT professionals to engage in conversations at various events, both formal and informal, leading to long-lasting and mutually beneficial connections with thought leaders. It provides access to research-backed material on issues that impact businesses and their stakeholders. Equally importantly, Gartner offers access to solutions providers. My interactions with such leaders were fulfilling and played a big role in honing my professional skills. The conference I addressed was attended by around 400 participants, all of whom held the senior-most positions in the IT industry.

Becoming a Marathon Runner

Moving to my new residence came with some immediate disadvantages. At my previous home, I had developed a circle of friends with whom I hung around in my free time. Now I had to start all over again in a new place. Fortunately, a few of my colleagues, mostly Indians, lived nearby, and I began socializing with them. Sriram, Vivek and Dustin were my colleagues at Infosys. Then Sirsij, Jeetu Gulati and Rajesh joined the group. We would visit the famous Kinuta Koen Park, which was more like a mini forest, on the weekend with our families. It had a jogging track, and we could also play games such as tennis and frisbee inside the park. It was barely 2 km from my residence, and it soon became our favourite weekend outing.

I also joined a tennis club and began playing some serious tennis with youngsters; Debangi was also a member. It also started my love for long walks and jogs. I began taking that sport rather seriously, beginning with 5-km runs. I moved to a higher level and participated in 10-km runs, an event sponsored by Citibank. With my confidence growing, I decided to participate in marathons. I began with the half-marathon and then graduated to full marathons, participating in the Tokyo Marathon (one of the most prestigious global marathon events) and completing the race. I don't know where the stamina and energy came from; perhaps it had to do with the strenuous physical exercises I had got used to during my childhood in the fields.

The marathons were good for my health. They added to my sense of discipline; I would have to wake up early, shed my laziness and brave the biting cold to go out for the run. Long-distance running also calls for patience and strategizing, essential qualities I needed in my profession as well.

I had another reason for taking up long-distance running. During my interactions with IT executives, I noticed that after some rounds of discussions on the profession, they would often talk about their recreational activities. Some would talk about golf, others about tennis and yet others about some other subjects. This added value to the person, and they were respected and taken more seriously. I realized

I also needed a talking point. So I began to tell the group about my exploits as a long-distance runner. It drew several remarks of admiration. Soon, I was regarded as more than just an IT professional.

A New Start

I mentioned that I had turned down offers from various leading Indian firms because either the pay was below my expectations or I was asked to relocate to Bengaluru. This did not stop me from continuing to apply. In February 2013, I heard from Infosys; I had sent them my profile. They wanted somebody to lead their product, platform and solutions (PPS) business in Japan. This was different from my area of expertise, but it was a chance to do something new and different in the IT sector.

Several rounds of virtual interviews were conducted, and I went to India for the final interview, after which I was selected. The salary they offered was not bad by Japan's standards. I accepted, thus heralding a new phase in my career. After I put in my papers, HCL's top bosses went on an overdrive to try to retain me. For instance, they offered to reconsider my salary package and address any other grievances I may have had. It was nice of them to make those overtures, but I had made up my mind. I felt bad about leaving an organization I had been associated with for more than a decade.

I do not hesitate to accept that it was during my stint with HCL that I became a SAP expert. As a senior HCL executive, I gained access to and learned from several top-notch corporate leaders. Due to the support I received from HCL, I could gain a foothold in Japan. HCL gave me considerable legroom to operate my business portfolio.

However, it was time to move on. Several members of my team in Japan were disappointed and sad that I had decided to quit. They wondered if they would be able to continue doing the work without my support. I ensured them they were at a good company; besides, I wasn't leaving Japan, so I would be available to informally help them if they needed my advice.

After the selection formalities were over, I joined Infosys on 8–9 April 2013. The company's office was in Roppongi-itchome in Minato, Tokyo. Roppongi-itchome is among Tokyo's upscale areas and has numerous high-end Michelin-starred restaurants, shopping arcades and world-class museums. Infosys's office was swanky compared with HCL's office. I had to undergo what was called an 'induction phase' at Infosys. It involved visiting the firm's development centres in various Indian cities and interacting with the key people there so I could understand the company's functioning and capabilities and become familiar with the personnel. I looked forward to my new innings, more so because it would be a change from my earlier SAP/enterprise IT-oriented work.

I visited India with my family. The first induction trip was in Bengaluru. I found some time off to make a quick trip to Mysore. The next destination was Bhubaneswar. Thereafter, I went to Kolkata and Chennai (I also visited the famous Tirupati temple with my mother and in-laws) and finally ended the induction with another visit to Bhubaneswar, but not before going to Hyderabad and Pune.

Six months after I joined Infosys, there was a major turbulence in the company. Shibu Lal had taken charge.[11] A few months later, because the company's stakeholders felt

---

[11]Punit, Itika Sharma, and Bibhu Ranjan Mishra, 'Why the Infosys Buck Shouldn't Stop at Shibulal's Table', *Business Standard*, 24 April 2014, https://tinyurl.com/muzm9a6j. Accessed on 23 February 2025.

that the company was not moving in the right direction and its revenues were being adversely impacted, Murthy returned to Infosys in June 2013; a year later, he stepped down as executive chairman and became a non-executive chairman and, thereafter, chairman emeritus.

I do not wish to go into the internal details of the leadership tussle and changes, but the fact is that Infosys's overall functioning was impacted. We could not set clear goals because the goalpost kept changing according to the new strategy with the new leader at the Bengaluru headquarters. Every new person who took charge had their own perspective regarding the way forward. I also visited the US (New York and New Jersey). I remember the biting cold I had to encounter. I made quite a few friends during my short stay.

Meanwhile, I was learning Infosys's different ways of functioning. At HCL, I had the freedom to take key decisions regarding my portfolio (of course, I would keep senior management in the loop). This ensured the work did not get delayed; it was one of the major reasons for the high client satisfaction I had achieved in Japan. At Infosys, there were challenges as far as taking decisions was concerned.

It was not long before I realized it would be difficult for me to adapt to this work culture and that it would destroy the credibility I had laboriously built over the years with the corporate sector in Japan. One day, I was told by senior management that they wanted me to set up Infosys's SAP business in Japan, even as the firm continued with its PPS portfolio. Infosys's SAP business in Japan was smaller than HCL's, although it was doing very well in the embedded software business. One reason why I had opted for Infosys was that I would be able to do something other than SAP, but now I was being asked to set up SAP while managing the PPS portfolio.

As I was contemplating my next move, there were some happy moments on the personal front. We celebrated Utkal Divas (Odisha's foundation day) with much fanfare in Tokyo. I also attended Deputy Chief of Mission Sanjay Panda's son's wedding. Another memorable occasion was the father–child breakfast interaction Debangi's school organized. Debangi read out something she had written for me; I was touched by the sentiment and the beautiful way in which she had written it. I was not aware she could write so well. The annual Lord Jagannath Rath Yatra was organized, wherein I played an important role. By then, the group that conducted the event had split into two. The other group held the Yatra outside Tokyo.

After nine months at Infosys, I decided to leave. I discussed the matter with my family and explained to them the disadvantages of continuing with the company. It was time to look for another opening.

10

Settling Down at L&T

When I decided to quit Infosys, I thought the short stint would adversely affect my profile. However, I had worked at HCL for close to 14 years, and I was confident this fact would weigh in my favour and negate any impression potential employers might entertain about my professional instability. I began looking for an opportunity and applied to TCS. Hari Bhat, my colleague from HCL, had become an advisor to L&T, the well-known engineering and construction company that had branched out to IT software and solutions and had a presence in Japan. On his advice, I applied to L&T, and he spoke about me to the management.

However, this did not mean I had an easy entry. I had to sit through multiple rounds of interviews. After the initial round of interviews with the APAC head and chief executive of L&T Infotech (LTI), I was selected to travel to Mumbai in February–March 2014 for the final interviews, which were conducted throughout the day by different people at different times: the IT firm's industry head and the managing director. As if this was not enough to gauge my expertise and usefulness to L&T, the company's board of directors also interviewed me. (Before the meeting, I had to listen to the company's anthem, which was mandatory before the board met.) The board was headed by the chairman, the greatly respected and well-known Mr A.M. Naik.

The group CEO, K. Venkateswaran, CFO, HR head and managing director of the IT business were also present. I faced a formidable team. They were all senior people, and nearly all were over 65 years old. This surprised me because the average age of the seniors I had been serving for years in the IT sector was half that. I felt like a child being hauled up before experienced adults.

Having cleared this difficult round, another challenge awaited me. I was then to be interviewed by A.M. Naik and the managing director of LTI. They asked the usual questions: my experience, salary expectations, etc. Naik was from Gujarat and a shrewd and tough negotiator as far as remuneration was concerned. I let it be known that I already had an offer from another reputed company. When Naik's deputy asked me why I had not accepted that offer, I told him I would do it in case L&T's salary package was not competitive enough. My candidness floored them because they did not ask me about money again. Out of the blue, Naik asked me if I had been asked to leave Infosys. I assured him I had quit voluntarily and that he could check with Infosys management. He let that subject pass.

Initial Challenges

L&T was an engineering and construction company, and its mindset and work culture were very different from those of the IT sector. There was substantial formality, with 'sirs' floating around.

After the interview, LTI Managing Director V.K. Magapu invited me to lunch in the canteen reserved for the senior-most executives, including board members. Naik was there, too. He asked his deputy about the Cloud: 'How is the Cloud business?' The LTI chief said it was a novel concept, but the size of the deals was small. I was amused by this talk. Here we had people in their late sixties and seventies discussing Cloud storage and Cloud computing. A twenty-something-year-old in the IT sector would have tutored them, although the Cloud phenomenon was a new concept then.

Later, the HR head questioned me about my school and college education. I later learned she was from Odisha. That may explain her interest in my background.

The L&T people wanted me to stay back for another day, promising that the formalities of my appointment would be completed by then, but I excused myself. I had to return immediately because I did not want Infosys to get suspicious about my prolonged absence. Three days after I returned, the final appointment letter arrived. As discussed, although the fixed component of the salary was almost the same as at Infosys and what I had been offered by TCS, the variable part was much higher.

I joined LTI in Japan as country head and area vice president in April 2014. Later, as part of the induction programme, I visited their main development centres in Pune, Mumbai (Powai's head office and Navi Mumbai) and Chennai. I decided to develop my core backup team in Chennai because key members for the Japan delivery were based there. In August 2014, I visited Las Vegas on behalf of one of our Japanese customers, Hitachi. It was a great experience; I took a helicopter ride and drove a Ferrari.

Before I joined, LTI had been split into two. LTI took care of product development and enterprise IT, whereas a new arm called LT Technology Service (LTTS) was engaged in the business of embedded technology (software embedded in a host of products as in automotives and mobile phones). LTTS had a chief in Japan, who was an old-timer L&T person. Because LTI and LTTS shared the same office, he was always throwing his weight around and seeking to take credit for everything. Before I joined, a senior executive from India would occasionally visit Japan to oversee the functioning of LTI.

I had my ways to deal with such complicated situations. Besides, the situation was nothing compared to what I would discover: LTI had just one client with decent revenue. I began wondering if I had landed myself in a soup, but there was no turning back; leaving immediately after joining was not an option. I decided to plunge into the new challenge and build the business from scratch. Our office was in the prestigious Yokohama Landmark Tower, then one of Japan's tallest buildings (972 feet high), in the Minato Mirai district. This was slightly inconvenient for me as I had to travel one hour by train each way. Our office building was on the 69th floor (which has an observatory); we could see Sky Garden, from where one can get a 360-degree view of the city, and, on clear days, Mount Fuji. When this iconic tower was inaugurated, it had the world's fastest elevators, reaching a speed of 41 feet per second; in other words, the elevator could reach our floor in roughly forty seconds. Several Indian IT firms had their offices in the tower. Within two months of joining, we moved to another floor and had a bigger space for our operations.

I began working 15–16 hours every day. In the first year, the challenge was sizeable. Even the personnel for the assignments in Japan came from India on deputation. Initially, I had to depend on seniors in India, but later, I was given more freedom. I also got busy with something I had not anticipated.

Narendra Modi's first visit to Japan as the Prime Minister of India took place in August 2014. A business delegation, which included our chairman A.M. Naik, also came. I had to arrange for his various meetings but had few resources at my command. Fortunately, I received support from some people within the organization, and we managed the logistics with the other senior management team based in Tokyo. Naik came and left on a chartered flight. Among the meetings scheduled was Prime Minister Modi's interactions with Japan's non-resident Indian (NRI) community. I had the fortune to attend the event and personally interact with him.

L&T had wide-ranging interests, such as engineering, construction, mining equipment and turbines, in Japan. Naik had a packed schedule with as many as eight meetings every day; he was in Japan for four days. I had to make the arrangements for those meetings, such as inviting the top corporate honchos and preparing briefs for the chairman. Several CEOs from Japan were eager to attend those meetings because they were eyeing the Indian market. I had a tough time finalizing the list of invitees. I had to put everything else on hold in the months preceding these events and concentrate on making Naik's visit successful.

Settling Down

My efforts did not directly benefit my business portfolio, but I scored many brownie points. The other advantage was the opportunity to meet and interact with several CEOs of Fortune 500 companies in Japan, build contacts and learn from their experiences.

Naik was very particular about everything—food, travel, stay, etc. He would not attend meetings with smaller clients or potential smaller clients; instead, I was asked to attend them. He reserved his presence for 'big meetings'. His visit was strenuous for me because he was a strict man and expected not a single mistake in any of his meetings. When he came for a second time, things were more relaxed. On his first trip, he was accompanied by Rajat Mathur, whom he introduced to me as my new boss (in charge of the Rest of the World, outside North America and Europe). I was taken aback. Naik was also accompanied by S.N. Ray, an L&T board member and his confidant. Rai had the habit of offering feedback to the chairman on nearly every subject.

I recall an interesting incident in connection with Modi's visit. Naik insisted I organize for him to attend the NRI meeting. I told him politely but firmly that such an arrangement was next to impossible because the interaction was for NRIs only. He then suggested I take Ray along. I had to turn down that suggestion, too. He reconciled to the situation.

On the personal front, I took the lead in establishing the Odisha Community, Japan, Tokyo (OCJT), of which I became the president and chief of strategy. We organized Ganesh Puja on Ganesh Chaturthi and the annual chariot festival in Funabori, Edogawa-ku. After the dust settled following Prime Minister Modi's visit, I was back to actual work, which essentially included ramping up LTI's business. 2014 thus went by.

The new year was full of challenges. All the existing clients, which were very few to begin with, had dwindled substantially. These clients were being served by people who came from India for the assignment and left. There was neither a sense of ownership among them nor were they concerned about the needs or satisfaction of our enterprise IT customers. Besides, they were not conversant with Japan's work culture and could not communicate effectively in Japanese. Consequently, the clients did not get good service, their long-term interests were not served by LTI and they disassociated themselves from the organization. So, our existing–existing (E–E) business had evaporated. There was no question of getting existing–new (E–N) businesses because the existing ones had gone away.

I was left with no option but to create a new customer base. Because I was well-versed in Japan and its work culture and had some standing based on my track record, I was able to get and nurture new customers. However, getting new customers was not easy. It would take me months, sometimes a year, after I had made several presentations and sales pitches to get clients to sign the agreement. I was focusing on enterprise IT, including IT services. In short, on-ground implementation would take years. By 2016, however, I had acquired a few clients and got assignments, even though they were small to begin with.

The top brass at L&T was happy with my efforts and success. They were especially pleased I had helped them get new businesses outside of my portfolio; as I said earlier, L&T had a major presence in Japan in construction and engineering. In those days, L&T's construction business was handled by S.N. Subrahmanyan, now the CEO and managing director of L&T and one of India's leading corporate figures. He was aggressively pushing for business in Japan, and I helped him in his efforts. That's how I got to know him well and developed a rapport with him.

He visited Japan at least twice a year. India (through L&T) and Japanese firms were collaborating on various projects in India, such as the Delhi–Mumbai Corridor and Metro Rail. I took care of the logistics of his visit, arranged for his meetings, prepared the agenda, etc. One day, he suggested

I also pitch my business to his clients in his meetings. I did that but got only a few customers.

L&T had its annual sales meets in Lonavala, near Mumbai, and I would attend them. It was a matter of satisfaction that my efforts were recognized and my profile grew in the company. Meanwhile, several senior company executives, such as C.S. Kakkal, the chief operating office; Rajat Mathur and Vaibhav, the global SAP head, visited Japan, and I had the opportunity to interact with A.M. Naik again in 2016 as he visited along with the new CEO, who announced and introduced all the key partners and customers of L&T group.

On the personal front, I had a trip down memory lane when I visited NIT-Rourkela in December 2015 for a gathering of the 1993 graduates.

11

Business Takes Off

I have already spoken of the challenges LTI had been facing in Japan when I joined and the efforts I made in reviving our business, working day and night against many odds. Naturally, I was thrilled when my firm received the Excel Partnership Certificate from Hitachi Solutions in the middle of 2015. I felt proud to accept the certificate on LTI's behalf. It vindicated the work I had put in over several months to win our clients' trust and satisfaction. Rajat Mathur, the chief executive of Emerging Markets, described the occasion as a 'proud moment for us at L&T Infotech…indeed a feather in the cap for L&T Infotech's Hitachi team.'[12]

Winning the certification was difficult. Hitachi Solutions began the evaluation for global vendors in 2012–2013 with various projects. We were evaluated on numerous parameters, such as global capacity and security and quality of services. At that time, out of Hitachi Solutions' 450 partners, only 37 were Excel partners. We were, therefore, immensely proud to make the cut. As area vice president (APAC-Japan), I

---

[12]'L&T Infotech First Indian IT Services Company to Receive Excel Partnership Certificate from Hitachi Solution', *ITWeb*, 20 July 2015, https://tinyurl.com/ycyt9y2n. Accessed on 23 February 2025.

received the certificate from Shigeru Kono, the executive and procurement head of Hitachi Solutions.

Kono said, 'This will enable Hitachi Solutions to not only leverage offshore services but also broaden the scope of our products and solutions. We look forward to a longstanding relationship by leveraging L&T Infotech's global presence and extend our market reach and services for the mutual benefit of both companies.'[13]

Meanwhile, some attritions continued at the senior level at L&T, though it did not directly impact my business in Japan. Mr Sanjay Jalona joined LTI as the CEO (from Infosys) around 2015.

Greater Responsibilities and Accountability

In 2016, a major development took place. LTI was listed on the Bombay Stock Exchange, and its initial public offering was oversubscribed, much to our delight. It was a milestone for our company, but it also increased our responsibilities. Now we were accountable to our several lakh shareholders, and we had to submit our quarterly performance sheet to the government as well as the stakeholders. In turn, it completely overhauled LTI's mindset and functioning. There was pressure on the senior management in India to perform, which percolated down to us. We had to become aggressive in getting new businesses, retaining existing businesses, improving our revenue flow, increasing our profit margins and cutting down costs wherever possible.

The company gave me stock options, which I could exercise in parts, to incentivize me to stay on. I was among the very few vice presidents to receive that option because

---

[13]Ibid.

it was not the firm's normal practice to offer stock options even to all area vice presidents. A.M. Naik, who was impressed with my work and whom I met during his trips to Japan, may have tilted the balance in my favour. However, I cannot claim with certainty that he suggested I be given the stocks.

As I slowly but surely began reviving LTI's fortunes in Japan, I got to work for our Japanese clients who had interests abroad and wanted me to take care of their IT/digital needs there as well. In 2016–2017, I visited Santa Clara in the US and Singapore on behalf of my clients. Soon after, I signed major deals with Japan's three big manufacturing companies.

I also struck an agreement with the France-based L'Oréal S.A., the internationally reputed cosmetics company. Today, it is the world's largest cosmetics corporate entity. L'Oréal had operations in Japan via its China office. So I visited China to pursue the business deal. L&T's presence in France and China proved to be of great help.

Our Japanese clients were keen on occasionally visiting India for two main reasons. One, they wanted to explore business opportunities in the growing Indian market. Some of them already had a presence and wanted to expand it, whereas others wanted a foothold. Two, they wanted to see the facilities we had back in India. They wanted to study our corporate functioning, the capabilities of our employees, etc. In Japanese terms, it was a 'Genmba' visit. As our customers, it was natural for them to want reassurance that their task was in capable hands.

Meanwhile, A.M. Naik and S.N. Subrahmanyan arrived in Japan in 2016. This was Subrahmanyan's first visit after he was officially announced as the next Group CEO after Naik decided to hand over the role. As with the previous visits, I was involved with organizing the logistics of their stay, multiple non-IT meetings, etc. Organizing meetings with our major clients and other corporate honchos was the major focus. Naik came with his wife and, like before, attended dinner meetings with only the big customers. He left with his wife soon after, whereas Subrahmanyan stayed back for a few more days.

We had a business lunch appointment, but A.M. Naik skipped the food because it was not vegetarian. On our way back in two cars, I was in the front seat next to the driver in a Mercedes Benz and Naik and Subrahmanyan were in the rear seats. Naik was a diabetic patient, and he was feeling weak because he had not eaten anything. We were on the lookout for a store where we could buy him a packet of potato chips. Finally, we found one. Both cars screeched to a halt, and we rushed out, leaving Naik in the car, to buy the item. At that moment, nothing seemed more important than purchasing a packet of potato chips. From the next day, I always kept potato chip packets in the car.

In Japan, the hotel check-in time is 3 p.m., and the hotels are strict about it; anybody who arrives before must wait till 3 p.m. to book a room. If someone wanted to check in earlier, they had to book the room for the previous day. In the present case, the L&T people at the Mumbai head office made the booking for the same day the two men arrived. I picked them up from the airport and drove to the hotel well before the check-in time, only to be told that they would get their rooms at 3 p.m. and not a minute before that. Subrahmanyan fretted and fumed while Naik was calm. Apparently, the company did not find it sensible to pay for the room a day earlier when nobody stayed.

Without checking into the hotel, we proceeded to a lunch meeting with the Indian ambassador at a top-end restaurant in a mall. Our vehicles were stopped a short distance from the mall due to traffic, and we had to walk some hundred metres, which infuriated Naik even more. To add to his woes, the food was not to his liking, and after business discussions, he thought the matter was over. He indicated to me that we should wind up the meeting soon.

During the trip, because Subrahmanyan had been named the CEO-designate, Naik briefed him about L&T's internal functioning, the politics, the key people, their conduct and attitude, etc. I listened while they spoke in the car; thus learning a great deal about L&T's internal working. Upon formally handing over the charge to Subrahmanyan, Naik spoke fondly about me and complimented me on the good work I had been doing when I saw him off at Narita airport. I felt satisfied and emotional because it was rare for Naik to openly praise an employee. I shall always be thankful to him, one of the greatest business executives in my opinion, for the innumerable learnings I gained from his visit.

Personal Issues

I faced an emotional moment on the personal front. My mother suffered a heart attack in 2017. In 2009, she had a stent implanted in her heart, and since then, she was well and active. I am not sure what triggered the stress that resulted in the cardiac issue. She had been staying with my sister, who was married and living in Jashipur. After retirement, my elder brother also settled down in our home town. There had been some land acquisition for the National Highway by the government for a road bypass and our land had also been acquired. We received a considerable sum of money. Had my father been around, he would have distributed the amount among my siblings without anyone raising objections. My mother may have found the task difficult, which must have added to her stress. She was treated by several doctors, including those in Bhubaneswar. Later, physiotherapy was recommended because she was paralyzed on one side due to the stroke. However, the treatment did not have the desired result. In 2019, she died of age-related illness at 81 years old. I stayed in Jashipur for three weeks for the various rituals. Unfortunately, Debangi could not be there for her grandmother's final rites because she was playing in an Asia-Pacific-level tennis tournament, which she won. My mother's demise was a great personal loss for me.

Back in Japan in 2016, Debangi had to stay for short durations in Hong Kong, Oxford (in England) and the US as part of an orientation programme for her studies. It was the first time she was away from us, so naturally, my wife and I were anxious. However, it was a good learning experience for her. In the summer of 2017, she went to Los Angeles for a training session conducted by the Center for Talented Youth (CTY), a non-profit centre of Johns Hopkins University. The CTY, globally considered one of the most prestigious programmes, delivers academic excellence and offers transformational experiences to advanced learners from grades two to twelve. It was founded in 1979 to foster intellectual growth in exceptional students from different backgrounds and communities and provide personalized guidance. Jaysree and I would pick her up and use the occasion for family outings to Hollywood, San Francisco, Las Vegas and the Grand Canyon.

Debangi did us proud by winning a national-level tennis tournament, the Tomas Cup. We also bought a new flat in Bhubaneswar. I participated in a road race called Yamathon. It was a unique kind of marathon wherein we covered a set route and, as proof that we had done so, we were to take photographs of the place and submit them to the organizers. Although participants cheated a lot, it was fun. I had been accepted as an entrant for the Yokohama marathon, but the event got cancelled due to a typhoon that struck the region.

Union Cabinet Minister Dharmendra Pradhan visited Japan on an official trip in 2017, and I was involved in making the arrangements, including organizing some meetings on skill development.

Business Begins to Grow

The hard work my team and I had put in since I joined LTI finally began to pay off in a major way in 2017–2018. We closed major deals in enterprise IT with reputed Japanese clients. I personally drove the sales accounts for three of them. Usually, agreements with Japanese customers are of short duration, but we managed to strike multi-year deals. I also had the opportunity to make sales pitches for a unique SAP enterprise solution, the S/4/HANA project. It was estimated to be a large deal to be carried out in the Time and Material Pricing mode, in which the client pays only for the time and resources spent on the project. It supports an agile development process.

The first such project began in June 2018, and it was one of only a few in Japan. Our clients included Ajinomoto, Yokogawa, Konica Minolta and Sojitz. Winning such deals against strong competitors such as Intelligence/NTT Data and Abeam was a great feeling. It took us almost a year to get the client's go-ahead, with multiple rounds of discussions in India, Japan and Singapore.

The years 2017 and 2018 also saw visits by senior L&T executives to Japan. Subrahmanyan arrived in 2018. Now as the Group CEO, he was more formal with me than during his earlier trip, but overall, it was a great experience. The same year, LTI CEO Sanjay Jalona also visited. The following year, it was LTI President Sudhir Chaturvedi's turn to visit from London. They were all quite satisfied and pleased with the upswing in LTI's business in Japan since I took charge.

An important event took place in May 2018 in Tokyo: the Wall Street Journal CEO Council meeting. L&T was a member of this group. The CEO Council helps members develop the right relationships and engage in off-the-record conversations with equals and corporate influencers. One can contribute through individual presentations and talks and benefit from peer experience and analyses. It was a learning experience to listen to the esteemed speakers, two of whom I still remember:

Masayoshi Son, one of Japan's leading investors in India, explained why and how he took barely 15 minutes to decide on investments. It was a revelation because we thought investors took months doing due diligence to decide instead of minutes. A Japanese billionaire and technology investor, he founded the SoftBank Group Corp. He was a controversial figure who had lost tons of money in his various investments during his career and was ranked 69th on the Forbes list of the world's billionaires in 2023.[14]

Christopher Weber of Takeda (a drugs manufacturing company) is known for having fought his way to an agreement with the Dublin-based Shire to take over the company. The Japanese company had a market value of just $33 billion, which stoked fears about how much debt it would have to take on to fund the acquisition. Analysts said Takeda was

---

[14]Singh, Sahib Preet, 'What Is SoftBank CEO Masayoshi Son's Net Worth?', *Market Realist*, 27 December 2023, https://tinyurl.com/ysan25mm. Accessed on 23 February 2025.

eager to acquire Shire to boost its global presence and get hold of its portfolio of rare-disease medicines, which have high profit margins.[15]

I also attended a Japanese global IT meet and a SAP Sapphire conference in Orlando, USA. Julia White, the then chief marketing and solutions officer and executive board member at SAP, said, 'Every organization, in every industry, wants to be "future-proof". Join our global community at SAP Sapphire to share what's already working and explore what's possible. "Future-proof" is a way of operating, and it can be built right into your business with SAP.'[16] In my subsequent visit to the US, I was able to meet the president of a leading Japanese company at short notice. The fact that I was based in Japan gave me an early appointment. Moreover, I was able to seize his attention and respect when I conversed with him in Japanese. As I said earlier, these are huge advantages for executives operating out of Japan. I thanked myself for learning Japanese and picking up the nuances of Japanese mannerisms, customs and traditions.

During one business trip to India with a top-level Japanese delegate, I told him my birthday celebrations were going to be ruined due to the trip. Imagine my surprise when the Japanese team organized a birthday celebration for me at JW Marriott Mumbai Sahar. This is what happens when you build a trust-based relationship with your customers. I visited the remote areas of Haryana and Rajasthan to look at the Western Freight Corridor being constructed by L&T

---

[15]Hirschler, Ben, Paul Sandle, and Sam Nussey, 'Japan's Takeda Clinches $62 Billion Shire Deal as Pharma M&A Rolls On', *Reuters*, 8 May 2018, https://tinyurl.com/3zawau29. Accessed on 23 February 2025.

[16]*SAP Sapphire | SAP Events*, https://tinyurl.com/pbbjdmy6. Accessed on 23 February 2025.

in collaboration with a Japanese infrastructure company. I also learned more about the upcoming Delhi–Mumbai Industrial Corridor.

Meanwhile, my obsession with tennis continued. At Seisen Tennis Club in Japan, I managed to avail the services of a reputed coach, Khalil from Malaysia, who also coached my daughter.

All in all, 2017–2018 was an immensely satisfying period for me, the exception being my concerns about my mother's failing health.

12

Consolidation and the COVID-19 Challenge

Business continued to grow in 2018–2019 as our hard work began to show results. I also received a decent increase in my salary. Ever since I joined LTI, I was so occupied with bringing the business back on track and with the visits by senior executives, including that of A.M. Naik, that I had no time to enhance my professional skills. Now, I had the luxury of doing that. Thus, I successfully completed the S4H100_05 SAP S/4HANA Implementation Scenario training in Singapore. It is a central tool that guides SAP implementation. Top L&T personnel continued to visit, and as before, I was closely involved with the logistics of arranging meetings for them in Japan and preparing the agenda for those meetings, although they did not always have to do with the infotech business. A board member of the group, Desai, came to Japan to meet with our Japanese partner, IHI, a reputed company engaged in heavy engineering activities. The products it offered were in the areas of resource, energy and environment; social infrastructure; aero engine, space and defence; industrial system and general machinery, etc.

L&T and IHI had a partnership to construct various heavy engineering projects in India, with Japan funding those projects. When Japan funds projects, the Indian firm must collaborate with a Japanese company to execute those projects. This is to ensure that the benefits of the collaboration also reach Japanese companies, which boosts its economy and employment.

Cultivating a New Profile

Besides such corporate visits, I also got actively involved in visits by Indian dignitaries that were not strictly corporate-to-corporate. Although I did not know it then, this new focus would later help me build a new profile from business-to-business to government-to-government and, eventually, country-to-country. Earlier, I had played a role in the visits made by Indian Union Ministers Arun Jaitley, Nirmala Sitharaman, Dharmendra Pradhan and Manohar Parrikar. I was now involved in an official trip by the vice chief of the Indian Navy. He had come to explore the possibility of a collaboration with Japan to construct submarines for India's naval requirements. I also called upon Sanjay Kumar Verma, who had recently taken over as India's ambassador to Japan, as part of my new profile-building.

One of my major involvements in the various initiatives taken by state governments in India was when I worked closely with a Gujarat government delegation that came to Japan in 2018 to promote the Vibrant Gujarat Summit. The event had been conceptualized in 2003 under the leadership of Narendra Modi, who was then the state's chief minister. Over the years, it has become one of the world's most reputed global summits for business networking, knowledge sharing and strategic partnership building for inclusive growth and sustainable economic development. Vibrant Gujarat has played a key role in tapping Gujarat's entrepreneurial spirit and the advantages it offers to investors and manufacturers, domestic and foreign, helping the state stand out among the most industrialized in India.

The team arrived in Japan to woo Japanese investors to Gujarat. Although Gujarat is a major investment destination for Japan today, in those days, it was Chennai and Manesar. They held several road shows and interacted with leading Japanese corporate houses. I accompanied the official delegation on many of their shows, which allowed me to develop contacts with the state officials.

I have mentioned the critical role understanding the Japanese language, culture and traditions played in doing business. I knew that if India had to grow its businesses in Japan, promoting the Japanese ecosystem in my home country was essential. So I sponsored the visit of a reputed Japanese language teacher, Kozo Yoshida, to India in December 2018. He went to several cities in India. Today, it comes as no surprise that Japanese language classes are flourishing in many Indian states. I would like to believe I played a part, albeit small, to that end.

I accompanied Yoshida to many places in India. We went to Odisha, including my home town and my in-laws' place. He loved the experience and was a keen learner. I took him to important temples, though he had to be content with seeing the Jagannath Puri temple from outside because non-Hindus were not allowed inside. I dropped him off in Jamshedpur but ensured his further visits were taken care of. He went to Gaya, Kolkata, Delhi, Mumbai and Goa.

I hosted a delegation of Odissi dancers in Japan as part of my new outreach to non-corporate areas. This included a few Japanese dancers who lived in India.

Meanwhile, L&T Group CEO Subrahmanyan made a business visit to Japan in 2019, and as always, I was at the forefront of organizing his meetings and ensuring his stay was comfortable. By now, I was fully familiar with his needs, demands, moods, and likes and dislikes, so the event passed peacefully. In February of that year, I travelled to my home town and paid obeisance to the family deity, Tarini of Ghatagaon. It was also a chance to see my ailing mother, who was bedridden. It hurt me deeply to see her in that condition, but little could be done. We had provided her with the best medical treatment available in Odisha. She died in October of that year.

In March, I was back in India, this time with a major customer from Japan. He was eager to travel across the country and understand its people and culture. He even expressed a desire to go to the Himalayas. His CEO had advised me to take him to the smaller towns and villages so he could return thoroughly educated about the country. The CEO considered it important to know and appreciate the culture, language and traditions of the country one did business with. The company he represented had a major presence in India and was involved in the manufacturing and operating of signalling systems for fast trains.

In April 2019, L&T organized a global customers meet in Orlando, USA, and because some of our major customers were invited to the event, I accompanied them. Despite being busy with business matters, we had a good time. I interacted with a range of L&T's customers and senior-most executives. An important professional development I was involved in occurred when we partnered with Oracle JD Edwards EnterpriseOne (JDE). It was an ERP software company. Very few companies in Japan had the capability to work on projects related to JDE. The collaboration gave us many important leads to expand our customer base. JDE offers a modern and user-friendly experience to customers with purpose-built applications aligned to individual user needs. Integrated with digital technologies, the approach helps increase productivity through smarter and faster work methods. It is a fully integrated ERP software suite that provides more database choices and deployment options, including on-premise, private cloud, public cloud or hybrid cloud for optimum flexibility. It has more than 80 application modules, end-user reporting and personalization capabilities.

Moments of Personal Joy

It was a trip down memory lane when I visited my alma mater, NIT-Rourkela, to attend an event marking the silver jubilee (25 years) of the graduation of my batch. I was accompanied by a close friend, Tapan Jena, and his family; my wife and daughter came along as well. We travelled by road from Bhubaneswar to Rourkela. Although the road was not in very good shape in certain patches, we enjoyed the journey. We stayed overnight in a guest house in Hirakud, where the famous dam is located. The accommodation had been organized by my friend and classmate, J.P. Nayak.

The event at NIT-Rourkela was marked by several functions, and there was much dance, music and merry-making. I took my family to see the hostel where I used to live and reminisced about the days gone by. I had the chance to meet several classmates who had spread across the globe to pursue their careers. I was in touch with some of them and met some regularly, but there were also those I was meeting for the first time since graduating. Before returning to Tokyo at the end of December 2018, my family and I visited the Sun Temple in Konark. It was a hectic but fun-filled trip.

Meanwhile, Debangi continued participating in major tennis tournaments across Japan, and our weekends were spent travelling with her on her sports and academic-related activities. She was chosen to be a member of Firebird Mei, a part of the Seisen Firebird Science and Innovative Team. As part of the team, she travelled to the NASA Kennedy Space Center in Florida, USA, to participate in the Conrad Challenge in the Health and Nutrition Division. There, the team displayed its invention, eSecure, a compact epinephrine auto-injector encapsulated in a thermally insulated smartphone case. Other teams in the finals were from Australia, India, Thailand, Nigeria, Singapore, South Korea, Qatar and the US. As parents, we felt proud of our daughter's achievements.

The most exciting event for us Indians in Japan was Prime Minister Modi's visit in June 2019 to attend the G-20 Summit in Osaka. He received a warm welcome from the Japanese, led by the then Prime Minister of Japan and his friend, the late Shinzo Abe. Modi had a packed schedule, with as many as half a dozen meetings in a single day. He held bilateral and trilateral meetings with several world leaders, including the Russian and Chinese Presidents. The theme of the meeting was Human-Centred Future Society. As part of the Indian and Indian business community, I went to meet him in Kobe around 600 km from Tokyo.

Meanwhile, I was able to achieve a long-pending goal: successfully completing the Yokohama full marathon (42.195 km). Incidentally, I received two medals that day: one for completing the September 2018 run and the other for the 2017 event that got cancelled due to the typhoon. It was fun to run in the Yokohama Bay area, even though I felt the heat during the last leg of the marathon. The 2018 event was organized by the Yokohama Marathon Organizing Committee (the main organizers), the City of Yokohama, Kanagawa Prefecture, the Yokohama Sports Association and others. The full marathon began from the Minato Mirai Ohashi Bridge and ended at PACIFICO Yokohama.

The COVID-19 Challenge

By December 2019, our business had not only stabilized but also grown. However, then came the COVID-19 pandemic. As we all know, the pandemic began in China and swiftly spread worldwide from the beginning of 2020. Over the next two years, it caused untold havoc, claiming millions of lives. Economies were destroyed, and normal life was disrupted beyond imagination. Japan was also affected by it. Based on the genome sequencing of COVID that hit Japan, the pandemic can be divided into different waves. According to the National Institute of Infectious Diseases, the first wave came from the Wuhan type that was prevalent in patients from China and East Asia, whereas the second originated from variants of the European kind (traced to early patients from France, Italy, Sweden and the UK). The third wave consisted of viruses carried by those returning to Japan from Europe and the US. Experts said Japan took a major hit from the European and US virus.[17]

Unlike countries such as India, Japan was slow to react to the crisis, but it did a good job of containing it.

---

[17]Van Damme, Wim, et al., 'The COVID-19 Pandemic: Diverse Contexts; Different Epidemics—How and Why?', *BMJ Global Health*, Vol. 5, No. 7, 2020, https://doi.org/10.1136/bmjgh-2020-003098. Accessed on 23 February 2025.

Interestingly, there was no mandatory lockdown, as we saw in many different nations, including India. Advisories were issued, and social distancing and wearing masks were made essential. Businesses that decided to shut down during the period were compensated by the government. Several small eateries managed by Indians closed down, their owners realizing that the compensation they would get from the government was as good or even more than the profits they made.

Fortunately, the number of fatalities in Japan was fewer than in other countries. That said, the impact of the pandemic was deeply felt in business circles. Japan depended on countries such as China and Taiwan for numerous products, such as semiconductors. Apparels were manufactured in countries like Vietnam and imported into Japan. Thus, although most factories and big business establishments remained open, their functioning was severely affected.

The pandemic resulted in serious problems for L&T's infotech business in Japan, which I headed. Forget getting new business; the challenge was to retain existing customers. I must add that we did not lose any of our existing customers during the challenging COVID-19 months. Because of the total shutdown announced in India, our offices back home, with whom we had close interactions in connection with the Japan business, were closed, and work from home started with adequate security in place. In Japan, my staff and I were wary of venturing out of our homes to meet clients, both existing and potential.

The traditional Japanese way of doing business largely depended on face-to-face meetings, and deals were agreed upon only after several such interactions. Now, such meetings had to be virtual. Our clients were uncomfortable with the new arrangement, and they felt uneasy about the work-from-home culture that had become a necessity during the pandemic. They were worried their data secrecy could be compromised. I had a difficult time allaying their fears and pointed out that the new work system was the only way out. I assured them that data secrecy would be protected and that in no way would efficiency be compromised.

Although initially reluctant, our Japanese customers adapted to the new work culture. They began considering outsourcing as a good way of doing business. Whether work was done in Japan or with India's work-from-home policy, they reconciled to the situation. The change in their mindset was good for us, and we did not disappoint them.

It took more than six months for the new arrangement to fall into place and for our clients to be comfortable with it. Business began to pick up after that. In fact, we started getting additional work. Customers were convinced we could manage issues of data secrecy, among others, while working from home.

I recall one hilarious outcome of social distancing and virtual meetings. It is common among the Japanese to get together to drink beer. Because face-to-face meetings had almost ended, a solution was found to continue the tradition. Alcohol was ordered online, and at an appointed hour, the group would connect, clink their glasses, and drink and converse virtually. To my mind, this was the ultimate proof that the Japanese had adapted to a virtual lifestyle.

I participated in an online session to address the students of Vinod Gupta School of Management, IIT-Kharagpur, in September 2020. I had done my business management course at IIT-Kharagpur, and addressing the students was an honour for me. The alumni committee that organized the lecture was kind enough to compliment me for the enlightening session. They said that my experiences with L&T and HCL in senior management roles were 'truly inspirational' and that my 'class notes in supply chain' were a 'lesson for us all'. The committee also lauded my advice that students must give equal attention and care to all subjects, explore new languages and set focused goals in life.

In 2019, a year before the pandemic disrupted our lives, I was a part of two important events. One was participating in the Saitama full marathon; it was my first appearance in that race. My professional engagements had kept me busy, and I had only two months to prepare, but I completed the race with my personal best timing. The second event was a students' reunion organized by my high school in Jashipur. I thoroughly enjoyed interacting with those who had been my classmates many years ago.

Meanwhile, in October 2019, my mother passed away. I recalled the love and affection she had showered on me, how she would put up with my whims and mischiefs and how she ensured I never went to school on an empty stomach. She would be up at three in the morning to prepare a solid breakfast of puffed rice for me, knowing I would skip dinner. I remembered every single moment I had spent with her. I visualized her happy looks when I used to meet her and how she would eagerly anticipate my trips to Jashipur after I had relocated to Japan.

I miss her as much as I did from the day she passed away.

13

Steering Towards a New Direction

The COVID years turned out to be of great significance for my family and me. In 2021, Debangi completed her school education and applied for admission to various universities in the US, UK and Canada. Considering her remarkable academic track record as well as extracurricular achievements, she received offers from many US universities, and she opted for the University of Michigan. It is a public research university that boasts eminent alumni, including several domestic and foreign heads of government, billionaires and Olympians. My wife and I were ecstatic that she gained admission to one of the best-ranked institutions in the world. The cost of education was high, and during that time, the value of the Japanese yen was considerably lower than the US Dollar, which really pinched me. However, I had decided to choose only the best for my daughter, who deserved it.

Initially, Debangi had trouble adjusting to the new environment, feeling somewhat overwhelmed. This was her first exposure to a truly international academic setup, and it was very different from what she was used to in her school life in Japan. The university was like a mini township, with students from around the globe. The campus was so large that vehicles ferried people from one end to the other. Over time, she adjusted to the new situation and did very well. For her first year, she chose Economics and Computer Science as her subjects, but in the second year, she opted for Computer Science as her major. She worked closely with Ross Business School's elite management clubs to get first-hand experience in consulting.

A Career-defining Decision

Throughout 2020, I did most of my work from home due to COVID-19 restrictions. This gave me ample time to think deeply about my career. I was doing well as the LTI head in Japan, and the salary and perks were good. Nonetheless, a sense of dissatisfaction was gnawing at me. I had, throughout my career, worked for others, and whatever achievements I had clocked were on behalf of my employers. I began seriously entertaining thoughts of branching out on my own and becoming an entrepreneur. I discussed the matter with my wife and daughter. They were encouraging but reminded me that if I took the plunge as an independent entrepreneur, I would have to say goodbye to a stable and successful career as an employee. I would no longer have the backing of a big corporate brand. However, if I was ready to take that calculated risk, they were with me.

Becoming an entrepreneur would not be a new experience for me. At HCL and L&T, I had virtually set up the businesses from scratch and had independent decision-making powers. In other words, I had been an entrepreneur all along. I was aware of the challenges and rewards. In case I quit, I would work for myself rather than for a third party. I estimated that even if I managed to draw in 10 per cent of the business I had secured for L&T in terms of revenue, I could manage my expenses and sustain my standard of living quite well.

I had another reason to branch out on my own. I wanted to tap into the growing digital services opportunities in India and work with industry and governments, state and central, to help talented youth, which India has in plenty, develop their skills. Besides SAP-related services, I saw enormous scope in the use of IT in healthcare and agriculture. There were obvious constraints to doing all that while I worked for someone else. My mind was made up, I put in my papers in March 2021. Hectic discussions with L&T broke out, but I was determined to part ways. In June of that year, I was a free man.

I took charge as CEO and president and as a partner of Inaho Digital Solutions (IDS). The company had been floated two years before (in June 2019) with three partners; I was the fourth. IDS aimed big. It wanted to primarily serve Japanese companies situated in and outside Japan and in areas as varied as manufacturing, pharmaceuticals, retail, telecom and media. Headquartered in Minato-ku, Tokyo, it was built with a capital of 39,000,000 Japanese yen. As the name suggests, it was engaged in providing digital solutions, including ERP (SAP), which was my domain. The company's name reflected its strong belief in the Japanese philosophy of business: *Minoru hodo koube o tareru inaho kana* (the more fruitful the ear of rice, the lower it droops).

Today, the company has more than 120 employees and offices in the Indian cities of Chennai, Coimbatore and Bhubaneswar and in other countries. It is a leading SAP and legal modernization service provider for Japanese clients in the global market. Back then, it was a small firm, a start-up. Initially, it was not easy to get business. Over the years, I built a rapport with many big corporate firms in Japan, and I believed my previous association would help me get business for IDS. However, we soon realized that the really big names were reluctant to associate with a small firm like IDS. We pursued them for months without success.

They were not convinced that given our limited resources, including manpower, we would be able to do justice to their requirements. Eventually, we changed our strategy. Instead of going after multibillion-dollar enterprises, we focused on smaller companies with a revenue of around a billion dollars. It was a wise thing to do, and over time, we managed to substantially expand our client base with the help of these customers. I would travel by car to attend client meetings because this made a good impression on the clients. I made another big decision that enhanced my stature in the eyes of my current and potential clients: I purchased a house. Owning a house in and around Tokyo is an expensive proposition, and I had successfully applied for a loan while still working at L&T. By the time I received possession of the house, I had left the company. If I were to seek a loan after quitting L&T, I would most certainly have failed at securing it.

Simultaneously, we focused on improving our human resources. We hired around 120 people, including some on a contractual basis, many of whom formed our back office in India. Remember, this was at a time when people in India were still working from home, and many had begun moonlighting, taking up freelance assignments while working full-time for one company. This naturally began adversely impacting their performance. It proved to be a challenge for us, and we had to struggle hard to overcome it.

We realized early on that it would be unwise for us to dabble in all the services that came under the SAP or digital categories. We were a small firm and had limitations. Thus, we concentrated on providing 2–3 key services in SAP and digital and ensured our full concentration was on delivering the best results for our customers. Some important clients demanded more than the 2–3 services we offered, and for them, we made an exception.

Being new and small, we had to convince potential clients of the advantages of outsourcing to us. I told them that one big advantage was that we could make decisions impacting their business in 30 minutes, whereas if they hired big firms, the decision-making process would be longer because they had a chain of command. The argument worked, and many companies signed agreements with us. The fact that I had a good rapport with the people at SAP, Japan, also worked in our favour because problems were resolved speedily.

IDS also concentrated on various other aspects to boost its presence. We hired experts to redesign our website (which hardly anybody knew about or visited), make it more interactive and ensure we got more hits. We wanted our potential and current clients to be impressed. We also got our company logo redesigned. We hired a consultant—a former HCL executive—to shore up our human resources and appointed HR heads in Chennai and Bangalore. We launched a drive to hire people straight out of the campus in India (Chennai, Coimbatore, Bhubaneswar, etc.).

That was not all. We had to conduct extensive and exhaustive training programmes for them and ensure they reached the desired levels. They were made to do crash courses in Japanese because nearly all our clients were Japanese companies. Some new recruits were trained in SAP and others in digital. We neither forgot nor allowed the recruits to forget that in the services business if we fail to provide satisfactory results to our clients, we would soon be out of business for that customer.

It took us almost 18 months to complete the training

process, and we had to spend a good amount of money. In fact, I am yet to get a return on investment on those expenses. Nevertheless, I believe IDS needed to make that investment because, without it, we would not have progressed the way we did in the coming years. It was the foundation on which IDS's future business was built. The good part was that our overheads were low because, as partners, we did all the sales and marketing in the initial months.

I visited India in March 2022 for the first time as the CEO and president of IDS. I went to different locations and interacted with the personnel we had hired. I was delighted at their enthusiasm and the fact that they had somewhat met my expectations.

In 2021, I turned fifty years old, and a big birthday bash was thrown to mark the occasion.

14

Focus on Odisha

With the creation of IDS, I was finally my own boss after having worked for corporate companies for nearly 25 years. It delighted me, regardless of the fact that IDS had to struggle for business initially to establish itself. However, my ambition would not stop at that. I wanted to use my expertise and position in Japan to do something tangible for India, particularly my home state, Odisha. I wanted to empower the state's youth by offering them employment opportunities using my Japanese connections.

This was not possible with just IDS, which provided digital solutions to Japanese clients. If I had to tap into the youth's potential, I had to first ensure they were adequately skilled to exploit the vast opportunities of the digital world. With this idea in mind, NITKAL (a combination of Nihon and Utkal) Enterprise Services was born in July 2022. Nihon is how Japan is pronounced and written in Japanese, whereas Utkal is Odisha's previous name. My first step towards working for business synergy between Japan and Odisha took shape with the formation of this Japan-based firm.

NITKAL is headed by my wife Jaysree and provides services in skill development. It trains its salesforce in various aspects, including Japanese language learning, and offers consultancy services.

Because I was fully occupied with IDS and Jaysree was keen to contribute to this initiative, she took the lead and I advised her from time to time. NITKAL's agenda was clearly defined. It would be an agency to promote employment by upskilling fresh graduates or those already employed but looking to enhance their skills in four primary areas: digital/IT, healthcare, agriculture and semiconductor and electric vehicle components. We would not be a training institution; instead, we would reach out to universities and other educational institutions, such as IITs and the Indian Institute of Information Technology (IIITs), and impart skills to their students. Thereafter, the trained candidates would either be absorbed by corporates or they could seek employment of their choice. In my role at IDS, I had limited experience in setting up teams in India. However, we had two clear objectives: to emphasize Japan-related employment and concentrate on Odisha, at least to begin with. With these in mind, NITKAL came to Odisha and began its activities.

Becoming an Enabler

We chose the four sectors mentioned above for our employment training programme or skill development with a purpose. Digital and IT solutions (which included Salesforce and SAP) were my area of expertise and were in demand in Japan. Because Odisha had an IIT and other technical institutions, such as the NIT and IIIT, not to mention universities that had courses in computer science, skill development in digital and IT solutions was a good choice. It made sense to tap into the Indian market. Consider the following: Japan lacks well-trained personnel in IT, and

India has abundant IT human resources; Japan's IT systems are ageing, and those in India are cutting-edge. Therefore, skilled personnel from India would not have difficulty being employed in Japan.

Japan has vast potential to employ healthcare professionals, especially medical attendants and nurses. It has a sizeable aged population that needs constant medical attention. For decades, such healthcare personnel came from countries like Vietnam, but they have been unable to meet the ever-growing demand. Moreover, the quality of their services was not always up to the mark as far as Japanese clients were concerned. I thought that India, especially Odisha, could be a good hub to identify healthcare workers and train them according to the needs of the Japanese market. The idea was to start with a few 100 in this profession and increase the number to 1000s over the next 4–5 years.

Agriculture was another sector waiting to be tapped. Japan imports much of its food grains (70 per cent of its requirements are met from outside Japan) and India was a good potential choice.[18] Farming in Japan is heavily mechanized. Back in Odisha, 60 per cent of the population was engaged in agriculture, but it had not been very productive—agricultural contribution to the state's GDP was just 16 per cent.[19] Keeping these facts in mind, NITKAL believed an opportunity for collaboration existed for India

---

[18]'Dangerous to Rely on Imports for Food Supply', *The Japan News*, 20 September 2022, https://tinyurl.com/2v6uephc. Accessed on 23 February 2025.

[19]Hoda, Anwarul, Pallavi Rajkhowa, and Ashok Gulati, 'Transforming Agriculture in Odisha: Sources and Drivers of Agriculture Growth', Indian Council for Research on International Economic Relations (ICRIER), New Delhi, Working Paper No. 337, https://tinyurl.com/27vxauaj. Accessed on 23 February 2025.

and Japan. People, even school pass outs, from Odisha could be trained in Japanese farming techniques so they could work there and be productive. Furthermore, the training could also be used when they returned home (for that was our plan). They could grow cash crops using the latest technologies, and over time, farming would become more productive in Odisha, leading to exports from India. There was a discussion in Japan about the immediate import potential of three products from Odisha: honey, ginger and garlic.

Finally, we wanted to skill the youth of Odisha in semiconductor and electric vehicle manufacturing. Both were high-tech sectors, and the issue of technology transfer from big companies in Japan to India would be tricky. Japan had burned its fingers with China and was wary of technology transfer even when it came to friendly countries such as India. Additionally, giant corporations, whether in the semiconductor business or electric vehicle segment, would be hard to bring on board because they had a long and tedious decision-making process. As far as NITKAL was concerned, there was no time to lose; we had already wasted enough of that. Thus, we consciously decided to talk to small firms, such as automotive component manufacturers.

We also discussed the issue with the government of Odisha and the Indian government. It helped that both governments had a progressive policy and were eager for Indian firms to team up with Japanese ones. The government offered a subsidy of 75 per cent (50 per cent by the central government and 25 per cent by the state government) for the establishment of such collaborative companies. I had many discussions with the Odisha government, technical institutions and National Skill Development Corporation (NSDC). I suggested that a special industrial zone be created in Odisha where these firms could operate. For example, there is one in Neemrana near Manesar. This would give a fillip to other developments as well, such as bigger roads, airports, hotels and restaurants, thus enriching the local economy. We also lobbied with the state and Indian governments to have a direct flight from Bhubaneswar to Tokyo. It is yet to happen. However, a private carrier began service from Bhubaneswar to Dubai/Singapore.

The decision to set up NITKAL was not made overnight. I have been working on the idea for months since leaving LTI. The groundwork involved finding the right teacher to impart education in the Japanese language, corporate culture and traditions. We needed trainers to conduct the courses and had to convince the institutions to come on board. Our target was to train around 10,000 youths over four years by tapping into more than half a dozen technical institutions and universities, primarily in Odisha.

NITKAL had no domain expertise in the four sectors mentioned earlier, so we needed to partner with firms that had experience in these sectors in India and Japan.

Booming India–Japan Relations

Governments and trade bodies from both sides have been working for a long time to increase business collaboration between Japan and India. They have picked a rapid pace in the last decade or so. Exchanges between the two countries are said to have begun as far back as in the fifth century when Buddhism came to Japan; with Buddhism came the Indian cultural ecosystem. Following Japan's devastation after World War II, diplomatic relations and India's iron ore went a long way in the revival of Japan's economy, and Japan, in turn, extended Yen loans to India, the first in 1958.

In August 2000, Japanese Prime Minister Yoshiro Mori visited India, and he and Indian Prime Minister A.B. Vajpayee agreed to establish a global partnership between the two countries. The India–Japan annual summit meetings have been regularly held since 2005. In 2005, when Manmohan Singh was the prime minister, the partnership was elevated to a 'global and strategic' one. The momentum was further boosted with Narendra Modi as prime minister when he visited Japan in September 2014. The partnership was elevated again, this time to a 'special strategic and global' level.

In December 2015, Prime Minister Shinzo Abe visited India and had a summit meeting with Prime Minister Modi. The two leaders resolved to transform the Japan–India Special Strategic and Global Partnership into a deep, broad-based and action-oriented partnership, which would reflect a greater convergence of their long-term political, economic and strategic goals. They announced the Japan and India Vision 2025 Special Strategic and Global Partnership Working Together for Peace and Prosperity of the Indo-Pacific Region and the World.

Modi visited Japan again in November 2016 for a summit meeting with his Japanese counterpart. This time, their vision statement reflected a commitment to working towards a free and open Indo-Pacific. In May 2022, Prime Minister Modi visited Japan for the Japan–Australia–India–U.S. Summit Meeting. More such visits and meetings were conducted. In recent years, the economic ties between Japan and India have only deepened. In 2021, India was Japan's eighteenth-largest trading partner, whereas Japan was India's thirteenth-largest trading partner. In 2021, Japan was the fifth-largest investor in India; by 2021, more than 1,400 Japanese companies had branches in India.[20] In 2022, Prime Minister Fumio Kishida visited India, and both sides resolved to promote bilateral trade and investment to higher levels. Notably, India has been the largest recipient of Japanese official development assistance (ODA) loans over the past decades, and nothing expresses India–Japan collaboration better than the Delhi Metro project. Japan and India are also committed to building high-speed rail systems in India by introducing the Shinkansen system.

With this background, furthering the relationship through skill development to make optimum use of the bilateral momentum becomes all the more critical. The Indian government incorporated NSDC in 2008 to promote skill development and employment opportunities. It provides funding to enterprises and organizations that offer skill training. It was estimated that by 2022, India would need an additional 104 million people in the workforce and 298 million would require an upgrade in training.[21] The NSDC signed a collaboration agreement with the Indian Institute of Corporate Affairs to train people in corporate social responsibility, corporate governance, business innovation, etc. NITKAL proposed to add to those efforts. We signed agreements with IIT-Bhubaneswar, the NSDC and IIIT to enable the skill development and eventual placement of the trained youth.

In 2023, NITKAL partnered with the Odisha University of Technology and Research to set up a dedicated skill

---

[20]'Japan-India Relations (Basic Data)', *Ministry of Foreign Affairs of Japan*, 12 November 2024, https://tinyurl.com/3er7hswe. Accessed on 23 February 2025.

[21]'India Launches Mission to Skill 400 Million by 2022', *Business Standard*, 16 July 2015, https://tinyurl.com/4phn2drm. Accessed on 23 February 2025.

development centre, which would cater to the burgeoning demand for IT professionals in Japan. We also began talks with IIIT-Bhubaneswar to establish a Japan-dedicated skill development facility. Many Japanese firms demonstrated interest in tapping into Odisha's human resource market. Fuji Soft Group, for example, proposed the establishment of a Centre of Excellence (CoE) in the state's capital city. The proposal was floated during Odisha Chief Minister Naveen Patnaik's visit to Japan and his interactions with major players in Japan's IT and IT-enabled sectors.

The future of India–Japan collaboration in various spheres, from business and trade to healthcare and IT, is bright, and I am sure we can play a role in enhancing that possibility. According to a research report published by the Standard Chartered Bank, India's GDP will nearly double in the next seven years to $6 trillion and per capita income will increase to $4,000 by 2030.[22] Japanese companies with advanced technologies could help create new jobs in India, whose government is looking to bolster the domestic manufacturing sector under the Make in India initiative.

One of the most important initiatives—a new buzzword—is global supply chain resilience. A Supply Chain Resilience Initiative was launched in April 2021 by the three Indo-Pacific economies: India, Japan and Australia. Bilateral cooperation in this regard underlined the annual summit meeting between Modi and Kishida.

Meanwhile, Odisha has taken several steps and continues to boost its role to this end. I am proud to say that NITKAL has been contributing to this effort. NITKAL aspires to help generate employment for thousands in Odisha in the next

---

[22]Joshi, Yathansh, 'Standard Chartered Report Predicts India's GDP to Reach $6 Trillion by 2030: Here Are the Highlights', *Swarajya*, 4 August 2023, https://tinyurl.com/2kem2356. Accessed on 23 February 2025.

four years and at least a few hundred in my native district of Mayurbhanj.

That the economic relationship between India and Japan has blossomed over the past few years gives me hope. According to Japanese government documents, pan-India trade from India to Japan went up from 739 billion yen in 2014 to 833 billion yen in 2022 and that from Japan to India rose from 861 billion yen to 2,018 billion yen in that same period. Direct investment from Japan shot up from 282 billion yen in 2014 to 471 billion yen in 2022.[23]

The overall robustness of the relationship between the two countries can be gauged from the fact that a host of agreements have been bilaterally finalized. For example, the agreement on the transfer of defence equipment and technology (2015); the agreement concerning security measures for the protection of classified military information (2015); the agreement on social security (2016); the agreement for cooperation in the peaceful use of nuclear energy (2017); the agreement on the reciprocal provision of supplies and services between the self-defence forces of Japan and the Indian armed forces (2021).

In a significant move, India and Japan signed a memorandum of cooperation (MoC) on 20 July 2023, to collaborate in the fields of semiconductor design, manufacturing, research, talent development and strengthening the chip supply chain. The agreement aims to foster government-to-government as well as industry-to-industry collaboration, with the establishment of an implementation organization to facilitate these efforts.

A key player in this collaboration is the Rapidus

---

[23]'Japan-India Relations (Basic Data)', *Ministry of Foreign Affairs of Japan*, 12 November 2024, https://tinyurl.com/3er7hswe. Accessed on 23 February 2025.

Corporation of Japan, a semiconductor manufacturer backed by prominent Japanese companies. At the time of writing, India was in advanced discussions with the company to expand the latter's presence in the country, thus creating a direct channel of communication at the government level between India and Japan. There is a big demand for legacy nodes in India, and by tapping into this space, India can cater to the Indian and Japanese markets.

The agreement is India's second major country-level collaboration in the semiconductor industry. Earlier, India and the US had signed multiple agreements to collaborate on semiconductor design, manufacturing, packaging and supply chain resilience. While US companies excel in manufacturing and packaging, Japanese companies lead in peripheral industries that produce the necessary chemicals and gases for semiconductor chip manufacturing.

15

Japan–India and Mayurbhanj

In the previous chapter, I mentioned that NITKAL's goal is to empower and skill the youth of Odisha to take advantage of the openings that exist in Japan–India collaboration in areas of agriculture, healthcare and digital/IT. Let me give you an overview of the possibilities and work we have been doing.

Agriculture

Japan meets a large amount of its food grain and vegetable requirements from abroad, so India can become an even bigger hub than it is today to meet such demands. For some of these products, Odisha can be a major destination for export to Japan.

Let us take the example of ginger. An indigenous plant, it is an important spice across the globe. It has enormous medicinal value. Furthermore, dry ginger is an ingredient used to manufacture oil, oleoresin, soft drinks and non-alcoholic beverages. India is among the world's largest producers of ginger—accounting for over 70 per cent of the production—and exports it to more than 50 countries.[24] Ginger happens to be one of the major crops cultivated in Odisha and exported to various nations. Its cultivation is largely concentrated in the districts of Koraput, Rayagada, Kandhamal, Gajapati, Mayurbhanj, Sundargarh, Keonjhar and Ganjam. Because ginger is cultivated organically in Odisha, it is considered to be of high quality. Additionally, the ginger grown in Odisha is milder, sweeter and less fibrous than the varieties found in other parts of India, thus making it easier to cook and use in pickles, curries and chutneys.

The global ginger and ginger processing market was valued at $2.16 billion in 2018 and was expected to go up to $3.42 billion by 2023. In 2019, the best-performing markets for Indian ginger per kilogram were Germany, the Netherlands, Australia, the UK and South Africa.[25] Japan has great untapped potential for ginger from Odisha. Koraput's spice has established itself in the international market, being exported to countries such as the US, UAE, Malaysia, Saudi Arabia and Nepal.

That said, ginger export from Odisha has to tackle many challenges, especially regarding the Japanese market. Although the quality of ginger is good, it is not consistently so across the state. This could be due to various reasons, such as weather conditions, disease and pests. Then there is the issue of adequate infrastructure for storage, transportation and packaging within the state. Without

---

[24]'Ginger Market Report by Product Type (Fresh Ginger, Dried Ginger, Preserved Ginger, Ginger Oil, and Others), Application (Food Industry, Pharmaceuticals Industry, Cosmetics Industry, and Others), Distribution Channel (Traditional Retail, Modern Retail Stores, and Others), and Region 2025-2033', *IMARC Group*, https://tinyurl.com/ytbtc3zz. Accessed on 23 February 2025.
[25]Ibid.

world-class infrastructure, farmers suffer damages and losses. Global competition is another challenge. Odisha has to compete with other major ginger-producing countries such as China, Nigeria and Thailand that have relatively robust infrastructure. Odisha's farmers must be prepared for price fluctuations in the international markets; here, the role of the state government in creating a cushion for cultivators during such eventualities becomes important.

The government can also provide the producers with the latest information regarding the international market's requirements so that the farmers can make informed decisions about when and where to sell. Cultivators have to be fully equipped with information about the quality standards they are supposed to meet if they want to tap into the international market. The state government can do more in terms of investing in infrastructure and technology or extending finance and credit to farmers to help them expand their operations. If the ginger produced in Odisha is to stand out from the rest, it needs to be uniquely branded and marketed.

Odisha must also compete with other Indian states. In 2021–2022, it was ranked sixth in the list of major ginger producers at 128.01 thousand tonnes, contributing 6.03 per cent to total domestic production.[26]

Turmeric is the other major crop with similar potential for export to Japan and the rest of the world. Odisha is one of the country's main turmeric-producing states, with the Kandhamal variety known for its strong flavour and vibrant yellow colour. Odisha was ranked sixth in domestic

---

[26]Keelery, Sandhya, 'Volume of Ginger Produced Across India in Financial Year 2022, by Leading State', *Statista*, 13 March 2024, https://tinyurl.com/2emckwjt. Accessed on 23 February 2025.

production in 2024.[27] Odisha has great potential to scale up its production and corner a large share domestically and internationally. Odisha's major turmeric-producing districts include Kandhamal, Koraput, Kendujhar, Dhenkanal and Rayagada. The Kandhamal variety is especially suited for large-scale exports. The major export markets for Indian turmeric are Bangladesh, the UAE, Morocco, the US and Malaysia. Japan can become a good market to tap into.

As in the case of ginger, there are many challenges for Odisha's turmeric, such as inconsistent yield and quality due to the use of traditional and not technology-driven farming practices, limited access to high-quality seeds and planting materials, and poor knowledge of sound agricultural practices and integrated pest management. Other usual problems relate to post-harvest handling issues, a lack of proper storage facilities and a near absence of value-addition. Access to testing facilities and accredited laboratories is limited. Farmers also face challenges in getting quality certifications (a must for exports) such as AGMARK, ISO, HACCP and GMP.

Let us take the example of millets. Odisha is home to a variety of these crops. Millets are climate-resilient, nutrient-dense crops that have great export potential, more so because global demand for nutritious, gluten-free and sustainable food products has been growing. By focusing on value addition, product development, market targeting, organic certification and strategic partnerships, Odisha can tap into this expanding market and position itself as a leading exporter of millets.

Millets are cultivated across Odisha, with the western and southern regions being the major producing areas.

---

[27]Keelery, Sandhya, 'Estimated Volume of Turmeric Produced Across India in Financial Year 2024, by State', *Statista*, 22 January 2025, https://tinyurl.com/452e9a7h. Accessed on 23 February 2025.

It is prominent in the districts of Koraput, Kalahandi, Rayagada, Kandhamal and Gajapati. Some finger-millet varieties cultivated in the state are GPU 28, a high-yielding variety with good resistance to blast disease and tolerance to drought, and VL 149, known for its high grain yield, early maturity and resistance to lodging. Little millet varieties include OLM-203, a good-quality, high-yielding and early-maturing variety suitable for intercropping systems, and OLM-11, known for its high grain yield, disease resistance and adaptability to Odisha's various agro-climatic conditions. Kodo millet varieties are CO 3, a high-yielding variety with good cooking quality and resistance to lodging and blast disease, and OKM-8821, a variety with high grain yield, early maturity and tolerance to moisture stress.

Millet exporters from Odisha may face many challenges. Limited global awareness about the nutritional benefits and diverse culinary uses of millets can hinder market expansion and demand growth. Smallholder farmers and decentralized production can result in an inconsistent and fragmented supply chain, making it difficult to ensure uniform quality and the timely delivery of millets. In addition, inadequate storage and processing facilities result in post-harvest losses, diminished product quality and increased costs. Issues of quality standards, market access, global competition, etc., also persist.

Honey is the fourth product from Odisha that has the potential to do well in international markets. The state has diverse agro-ecological conditions with mountains, rocks, rivers, waterfalls and many species of fauna and flora. Honeybees collect pollen and nectar from flowers like niger, mustard, sesame, sunflower, safflower and other crops, fruits and vegetables. They visit the flowers of creepers and various thorny, medicinal and fodder plants.

Honeybee activity has been observed in Cuttack, Jagatsinghpur, Jajpur, Kendrapada, Bhadrak, Balasore, Puri and Ganjam districts due to the availability of foraging plant species. Bee activity commences from October onwards. Odisha has five major honeybee species: Indian hive bee (*Apis cerana indica*), stingless bee (*Trigona iridipennis*), Italian bee (*Apis mellifera*), rock bee (*Apis dorsata*) and little bee (*Apis florea*).

India's honey production touched roughly 1,33,200 metric tonnes in 2021–2022, thus making it second only to China in the world. India is also one of the world's top honey exporters; it exported 74,413 metric tonnes of honey in 2021–2022, which fetched a revenue of ₹1,221.17 crore. About 12,699 beekeepers are currently registered with the National Bee Board. It has 19.34 lakh honeybee colonies. However, in 2021–2022, Odisha did not feature in the list of 10 major exporting states (Haryana topped the list); it was ranked 16th with 1.65 metric tonnes produced and just a 1.35 per cent share in domestic production. The positive takeaway is that it indicates a vast opportunity for the state to work towards becoming an exporter.[28]

Some hurdles must be crossed first. Beekeepers in Odisha lack technical knowledge and efficient management skills. There is also a scarcity of genetically superior bee species and a lack of infrastructure required to provide forward and backward linkages in the supply chain, and the honey gathered is of poor quality. These are drawbacks at the national level and are not limited to Odisha, but if Odisha's beekeepers are to break these shackles, they require the support of the state government and a drive to be the best.

---

[28]Husain, Asjad, 'Honey Exports: The Hunt for India's Sweet Spot', *India Business & Trade*, 7 May 2023, https://tinyurl.com/bdfkjy6b. Accessed on 23 February 2025.

AI and Robotics

We submitted a detailed proposal to the Odisha government for the establishment of CoEs for artificial intelligence (AI) and robotics. Many organizations across India have been facing a skill gap in AI and robotics, with some having an extreme shortage of niche skill sets, such as data scientists. Thus, organizations have begun simultaneously investing in the acquisition of fresh talent and AI-skilling their existing workforce.

Acquiring AI and robotics talent through hiring or outsourcing can only address the short-term skill deficit. Such skills will remain in high demand, so they will be scarce and expensive to source externally in the long run. As AI and robotics proliferate, companies that re-skill and train existing employees in AI will realize significant competitive gains. This is where we come in. Our training module will give opportunities for students to be deployed on a global scale, including via internships. It will lead industry collaboration and support the joint development of solutions through AI for different solutions.

Overall, the CoE would help increase the employability of university graduates initially in the 100s and, after two to three years, in the 1000s. It would help enhance current salary levels by 30–50 per cent. The CoE can become an innovation hub in Odisha. NITKAL could provide the Japanese experience and industrial visits to study Japanese know-how and skills.

Training in Japanese

We help students with JLPT to enhance their employability in Japan. The certification is given by the Japan Foundation and is internationally validated. The examination is held twice a year at various centres in India.

We provide all materials related to the course and conduct periodic tests to help students improve and focus on the listening, speaking, reading and writing aspects of the language. Classes are conducted in a hybrid mode (in-person and virtual) with a focus on team and individual improvement. The course covers introduction to Japanese language and culture, basic grammar, sentence formation, vocabulary and other similar subjects. After completing this course, a person would be able to speak basic Japanese.

Establishing Training Centres in Odisha

We also proposed setting up training centres in Odisha to augment the current training. Such centres would address the issues of visibility, business process training after basic IT training and creating e-commerce portals to sell products developed during training.

Many physically challenged people face a skill gap, with some having an extreme shortage of the right skills needed to get employment. To provide additional opportunities for employment, some areas considered are as follows:

New devices and trainers from Arrows Opthalmic: Acquiring devices from our partner company in Japan, based out of Osaka, which deals in medical devices, such as easy-vision for visually impaired persons to improve their reading capability and similar devices for hearing-impaired persons in Odisha, will be considered. Physiotherapist training will be imparted by a specialist for four weeks. This strategy has been successfully leveraged for visually challenged people in Japan. We proposed starting with a small batch of 10–12 students, which will be increased based on the outcome.

Business process and IT training: Initially, business process management will encompass training related to business process management lifecycle, business process management technology, value process management and human interaction management. It will have a train-the-trainer approach and hand over within one year. The training will last for six–eight weeks. Subsequently, IT skills training related to ERP will last for four–six weeks. After on-the-job training, some of the trained personnel can be considered for the role of ERP consultants; accordingly, additional training shall be imparted. They can then be placed within India or in Japan.

E-commerce portal: To streamline this process and reduce development and maintenance costs, we will design a no-code, user-friendly e-commerce platform. With our platform, any business or merchant can establish an online store in a few minutes, allowing them to quickly start selling products under their own brand.

Healthcare Training

The demand for skilled healthcare personnel is unprecedented in Japan, which faces an issue of population ageing. More than 29 per cent of Japan's population is over 65 years old—the world's highest proportion of the aged.[29] A report by McKinsey stated that Japan's working-age population will decline from 79 million in 2012 to 71 million in 2025 and its dependency ratio will rise from 0.60 to 0.73 during the same period.[30] There are not enough

---

[29]Chiba, Takuro, 'Japan's Elderly Population Climbs to Record 36.25 Million', *The Asahi Shimbun*, 16 September 2024, https://tinyurl.com/432z7sd2. Accessed on 23 February 2025.
[30]Adachi, Misato, Ryo Ishida, and Genki Oka, 'Japan: Lessons from a

young people in Japan to fill this vacuum due to the decline in its fertility rate. Given the nation's ageing issue and shrinking population, the resultant labour shortage must be urgently addressed. Japan's government has adopted certain measures such as premiums for the employment of older workers and raising the mandatory retirement age, among others.

The Technical Intern Training Program (TITP), established in 1993, promotes the skilling of foreign human resources. The Indian Ministry of Skill Development and Entrepreneurship has also initiated several measures. One such measure is signing an MoC with Japan's Ministry of Justice, Ministry of Foreign Affairs, and Ministry of Health, Labour and Welfare. The MoC was signed on 17 October 2017, to significantly expand bilateral cooperation between India and Japan in the skill development sector. Under the programme, selected candidates from India complete an internship for 3–5 years in Japan, after which they are required to return to India and utilize these skills. In January 2018, MSDE appointed NSDC to monitor the programme.

The opportunities for skilled Indian personnel in the healthcare sector in Japan can be understood from the fact that the projected number of vacancies (as of March 2023) was quite high (according to a study we conducted). Our organization endeavours to tap into this potential and make the youth of Odisha skilled to exploit these opportunities in Japan.

Hyperaging Society', *McKinsey Quarterly*, 1 March 2015, https://tinyurl.com/5n977t87. Accessed on 23 February 2025.

My Mayurbhanj

Over time, and more so after I became an independent entrepreneur and turned my attention towards Odisha, the thought of contributing to my home district of Mayurbhanj took root. I believe it is a debt I must repay, though I am aware I cannot fully do so, no matter how much I try. My journey, after all, began from here. I lived in Mayurbhanj for decades before shifting base and have seen its people, their potential and the potential of the region to grow. Now that I have the opportunity, I strongly feel I have to do my bit.

Mayurbhanj's economy depends on agriculture, which, in turn, depends on the climate and soil type. The main crop is paddy, followed by pulses and oilseeds. Although there has been a decrease in the cultivation of Kharif paddy in the last few years, the area under pulses, oilseeds and other cereals has increased due to the diversification of the crop pattern. The region is landlocked and lies in northeastern Odisha. Its geography is defined by the Similipal forests that surround the Similipal Hills and cover more than 25 per cent of the district's area.

Budhabalanga is the main river of Mayurbhanj. Originating from the Similipal Hills, it forms a waterfall at Barehipani on a northward course. It then turns southeast and flows between steep banks and sandbars. Baripada and the ancient capital of Haripur are situated along its banks. The climate is sub-tropical and marked by high humidity and monsoon rainfall. The average annual rainfall is around 164 cm; thus, the region is conducive to agriculture and agriculture-related activities. My focus on the agriculture productivity improvement approach with Japanese know-how can be used to some extent.

I plan to set up an IT development centre in my home

town of Jashipur. It will have a modest beginning, with around 40–60 people from the local population who will be trained and employed. Over time and depending on the response we get, the numbers can be scaled up.

Although my firm is not directly involved in the tourism industry, I would love to promote Jashipur and the rest of Mayurbhanj to domestic and international tourists. More than five beautiful waterfalls are located near Jashipur. Barely 50 km from the town is the famous Similipal National Park and a tiger reserve. Additionally, the Crocodile Park on the Khairi Bhandan River—also known as Ram Tirtha—is only 3 km away. It is the only crocodile nursery park in India.

There is good connectivity to cities such as Bhubaneswar, Cuttack and Rourkela from Jashipur. Furthermore, there is talk about constructing an airport in Baripada, Mayurbhanj, which will help tourists reach this place directly. An airport alone will not do. We need good-quality hotels and resorts, restaurants and fast internet services. I am certain that with holistic development, Mayurbhanj will emerge as a major destination on the international tourism map. To that end, I am already in conversation with various agencies in the tourism sector and would be willing to be a facilitator.

The ICIJ Connection

Along with being personally involved in many initiatives taken to forge a deeper connection between Odisha and Japan, I have benefited from various trade organizations that have been active in enhancing India–Japan economic relations. One such body is ICIJ, of which I am one of the directors. The ICIJ is a prestigious body that completed 100 years in 2021. A non-profit association, it is affiliated with several major industry and commerce institutions and holds membership to several large corporate groups with business interests in Japan and other countries. As an apex body, it fosters commerce and industry, friendship, goodwill, economic and cultural exchanges, and mutual understanding between India and Japan.

It has interacted with several esteemed dignitaries and guests and hosted them at various events and trade fairs. The ICIJ's forte is its ability to move with the times, anticipate the needs of the future and suggest proactive measures.

16
Unlocking Odisha's Potential

Odisha is one of India's fastest-growing economies. There are many reasons for this progress, but the most important are political stability and the vision and implementation of programmes by the state government led by Chief Minister Naveen Patnaik, who led the state from 2000 to 2024. Patnaik deftly managed welfare programmes so that they reached the poor and the needy and ensured industrialization through industry-friendly policies. In pursuing both, his government has taken care to emphasize multiple sectors, such as agriculture, tourism and mining.

Agriculture and Fish Production

Various annual economic surveys of Odisha have spoken of the achievements, opportunities and challenges for the state to grow in various sectors. The figures given in the following paragraphs have been taken from these surveys and government documents.[31]

---

[31] Planning & Convergence Department, Government of Odisha, https://tinyurl.com/yr9y89su. Accessed on 23 February 2025.

According to some estimates, the size of Odisha's economy has increased by over 127 per cent in the last six years in terms of gross state domestic product (GSDP). In that period, the state registered an annual average growth rate of over 6 per cent. This success hasn't gone unnoticed across the country, making it one of the top destinations for foreign direct investment (FDI). In the fiscal year 2011–2012, for instance, the state attracted investment proposals worth over ₹49,000 crore. In 2012–2013, according to the Reserve Bank of India, it got new FDI commitments worth ₹53,000 crore. In some phases, the GSDP dropped due to extraneous reasons. For example, in 2013–2014, it fell by a little over 2 per cent due to the Phailin cyclone; the cyclone led to a negative growth of over 9 per cent in the agricultural sector, besides impacting other areas. That said, the state's GSDP has shown consistent growth over the past decades. In 2001–2002, soon after Patnaik took charge, it was ₹46,756 crore; by 2022–2023, it stood at ₹7,65,962 crore.

As per the 2011 census, 61.8 per cent of the working population was engaged in agricultural activities, and yet, agricultural activities contributed just 16.3 per cent to the GSDP in the fiscal year 2013–2014, estimated to be 15.4 per cent in 2014–2015. This figure only shows the vast untapped potential in the sector. According to available statistics, the area under cultivation was 5,691 hectares in 2005–2006, and it fell to 5,424 hectares in 2013–2014. Rice is the dominant crop in Odisha, grown in 77 per cent of the area under cultivation. Odisha produced 8,360 metric tonnes of rice in 2013–2014, a drop from 10,210 metric tonnes due to Cyclone Phailin.

Odisha's agricultural contribution to the nation cannot be underestimated. For example, its national share in cowpea production was 45 per cent; in pumpkin, 33.6 per cent; in niger seed, 30.5 per cent; in turmeric, 17 per cent, and in san hemp, 24.7 per cent. The production of woodgrains has also risen over the decades. In 2011–2012, the total food grain production was 6,316 metric tonnes; in 2018–19, it rose to 9,251.54 metric tonnes.

The state government has been making continuous efforts to divert more paddy areas to non-paddy crops, which explains the negative compound annual growth rate (CAGR) in paddy cultivation (–1.10 per cent during 2019–2020). There has been a significant growth in the CAGR for the area under pulses. According to the state's economic survey for 2020–2021, it was 18.40 per cent, whereas it was just 3.98 per cent for total food grains constituting cereal and pulses. Again, the CAGR for the area under groundnut was 33.12 per cent and 23.22 per cent for oilseeds. The share of the area under vegetables increased from 7.42 per cent in 2014–15 to 8.24 per cent in 2019–2020, whereas the share of fruits increased from 3.63 per cent to 4.14 per cent in the same period. The significant share of 'other crops' indicates the rise of crop area under high-value crops like cotton, fibres and spices.

According to the economic survey, the government has been continuously taking initiatives for the diversification of crops, with emphasis on high-value crops like cotton, pulses, oilseeds, vegetables, spices and fruits, through various developmental schemes like National Food Security Mission, Integrated Farming System, Intensive Agriculture Programme, Mission for Development in Horticulture, Technology Mission on Cotton, Technology Mission on Sugarcane, and crop-oriented programme for pulses and oilseeds, etc.

The state launched the Bhoomihina Agriculturist Loan and Resources Augmentation Model (BALARAM) scheme with NABARD for sharecroppers in the field of agriculture credit in July 2020. The government of Odisha also launched the SAMRUDHI Agriculture Policy 2020; it emphasizes diversity, market linkage, value chain and technology. Other flagship schemes like Krushak Assistance for Livelihood and Income Augmentation, Mukhyamantri Krushi Udyoga Yojana, Odisha Millet Mission and Farmer Producer Organisation Policy are being implemented by the government for the welfare of farmers.

Odisha is also India's fourth-largest shrimp-producing state. Bearing this in mind, in 2017, the state government launched the Nabakrushna Choudhury Seccha Unnayan Yojana to provide irrigation facilities to about 55,000 hectares of agricultural land across Odisha. The scheme was implemented with an outlay of ₹635 crore over a period of three years. Under the scheme, for 46,296 hectares, 14 major and medium irrigation and 284 minor irrigation projects were revived. According to data from the Department of Animal Husbandry, Dairying and Fisheries, fish production nearly doubled from 3,81,828 tonnes in 2011–2012 to 7,58,960 tonnes in 2018–2019.

Industrial Growth and Power Generation

The main industries in Odisha are manufacturing, mining and quarrying, and construction. Most of the state's industries are mineral-based. Odisha has 25 per cent of India's iron reserves and 10 per cent of the country's production capacity in steel. It is the country's leading aluminium-producing state. At one point, mining contributed an estimated 6.31 per cent to the GSDP. At the same time, I believe there is significant scope to improve the state's business climate. The number of MSMEs, for example, fell from 69,673 units in 2018–2019 to 57,651 units in 2019–2020; investments in the sector went down from ₹3,19,656.45 (in lakhs) to ₹2,80,608.61 (in lakhs). Consequently, the number of people employed in MSMEs declined from 1,91,770 in 2018–2019 to 1,59,770 in 2019–2020. In the Ease of Doing Business Index (based on the implementation of the Business Reforms Action Plan recommended by the union government's Department of Industrial Policy and Promotion), Odisha's rank plunged from 7 in 2015 to 11 in 2016, 14 in 2017 and 29 in 2019. Clearly, a lot needs to be done, but the state government is on the right track, and the issue should be fixed soon.

Industrial development is the engine of economic growth. It leads a state's developmental change, constituting 36 per cent of states' gross value added (GVA) relative to 26 per cent at the all-India level as of 2020–2021. As per the 2019–2020 revised estimate (RE), the industrial sector grew 3.61 per cent in Odisha compared with 0.92 per cent at the national level. This is largely due to the large share of the mining sector. The annual average growth rate of the industrial sector in the last nine years was 5.36 per cent, which compares well with the national average of 3.77 per cent. The state accounts for 96 per cent of the country's chromite, 92 per cent nickel, 51 per cent bauxite, 33 per cent iron ore, 43 per cent manganese ore and 24 per cent coal reserves as of 1 April 2019. Odisha contributed around 25 per cent of the total major minerals produced in the country. The mining revenue collected during 2019–2020 was ₹11,020.02 crore, a 90 per cent growth over 2015–2016.

In terms of power generation, Odisha was the first state in India to reform its power sector. In 1996, it passed the Orissa Electricity Reform Act to restructure and privatize the sector. Before this legislation, the Orissa State Electricity Board (OSEB), the only public-sector company, had been producing and supplying electricity in the state since its establishment. However, by 1994–1995, OSEB had run into heavy losses; the gap between consumption and production went as high as 45 per cent.

This crisis propelled the government to undertake dramatic reforms that unbundled power generation from transmission and distribution. Hydropower plants were handed over to the Odisha Hydro Power Corporation, and existing thermal power plants were transferred to the Odisha Power Generation Corporation. Furthermore, the Grid Corporation of Odisha was made responsible for supplying power. In August 2014, the state government announced a plan to invest ₹54,000 crore in the power sector over the next five years to provide 24-hour electricity to the urban and rural parts of the state, firmly placing it on the path to becoming a power-surplus state. In 2018–2019, Odisha had an installed power capacity of 5,540 MW, and the per capita power availability in that period was 757.6 KW/hour.

The Services Sector

The state's track record in enhancing the services sector has also been good, and it outperformed many other states in the country, especially under Naveen Patnaik's leadership. The service sector contributed an estimated 51 per cent to the GSDP in 2014–2015. The primary sub-sectors, community and social and personal services, contributed 13.45 per cent. Trade, hotels and restaurants contributed over 13 per cent, whereas financial and insurance services contributed 13.64 per cent.

Odisha also has a well-developed banking network. There is one bank branch for every 12,000 people, and 90 per cent of the branches are in rural areas, thus effectively catering to the predominantly rural population. By 31 March 2020, as many as 3,089 public sector bank branches and 918 private bank branches existed across the state. Additionally, there are branches of small finance banks, cooperative banks, etc., all of which took the number of bank branches to 5,450 by the financial year ending 2020.

Improving the Lives of the Urban Poor

The state has won the World Habitat Award, a global recognition of its ambitious Jaga Mission. It is working to transform the lives of the urban poor by providing liveable habitats. The state government has also embarked on an ambitious 'Drink from Tap' mission under the SUJAL programme.[32] Odisha is the first state to launch this programme. It aims to provide a 24×7 drinking water supply to all urban households through metered connections.

Bhubaneswar became the first Indian city to achieve 100 per cent household water supply connections. In 2019–2020, a pilot study was initiated in eight zones across two urban local bodies (ULBs) (Bhubaneswar and Puri), covering approximately 22,000 households and a population of 1.2 lakh urbanites. Through Jal Jogan Melas, the government decided to cover all ULBs in the state to achieve 100 per cent coverage of all urban households under the Piped Water Supply Scheme by providing new connections in the project area and waiving connection fees for the urban poor (where distribution networks have been laid and where the distribution network exists but sufficient connections have not been given).

---

[32]G. Mathi Vathanan, *People First: How Odisha's Drink from Tap Mission Quenched Every Thirst*, Rupa Publications India, New Delhi, 2024.

Tourism

In the decades after India's independence from foreign rule, Odisha has made significant progress in emerging as a major tourist attraction domestically and internationally. The progress since 2000, especially in the last six years or so, has been rapid. One reason for this is the state government's enhanced financial and budgetary support to the tourism sector. I strongly believe the state's economy can rise higher if the tourism industry continues to receive sustained backing in terms of policies and their implementation. In this regard, it is heartening to note that the budget for the state's Department of Tourism was around ₹660 crore, up from the meagre ₹2.67 crore in 2000–2001; it is a whopping 24,619 per cent increase.

The state registered 1,53,07,637 domestic tourists and 1,15,128 foreign tourists in 2019. Compare this with 28,88,392 domestic and 23,723 international tourists in 2001, and one can understand how significantly the tourism sector in Odisha has grown. What has caused this massive increase? After all, important places of tourist interest have existed for decades in the state. There are several factors responsible for this phenomenon. The quality of the road network has dramatically increased; major cities are well-connected by air to important destinations within the country and abroad; a robust law and order situation; increased levels of skill development, and the government promoting the state as an investment and tourist destination, with an emphasis on ecotourism.

The state government has signed memorandums of understanding (MoUs) with various institutions to promote tourism. District tourism promotion councils (headed by district collectors) have been established, and agreements with self-help groups (SHGs) to boost tourism-related economic activities have been developed. Odisha Tourism Policy 2022 provides a concrete and realistic roadmap to develop tourism in the state.

Despite the COVID-19 pandemic, the state witnessed a domestic footfall of 37,42,221 and an international footfall of 2,269 tourists in 2021. A similar bounce back has been seen after the state gets hit by natural calamities such as cyclones. Today, most major and international brands in the hospitality and amusement parks' sectors have a strong presence in Odisha. In the last few years alone, these organizations have invested over ₹5,000 crore in the state. India's leading amusement park brand, Wonderla, has opened its fourth amusement park in Bhubaneswar.

However, a lot more remains to be done, and the state government is aware of that. For example, the highly successful responsible glamping festival, Eco Retreat Odisha, was expanded from one location in 2019 to seven unique ecotourism destinations in 2022. The three-month glamorous camp, developed to promote the state's rich culture and biodiversity, has an environmentally sustainable model that incorporates best practices in material utilization, zero liquid and sewage discharge and holistic waste management. Water-based recreation was launched at the Tampara Lakefront Project in Ganjam and Silver City Boat Club on the Mahanadi River in Cuttack, which provides tourists with recreational facilities using kayaks, jet skis, banana boats, etc. Cruise tourism is another niche water-based recreation project Odisha is working on. Odisha's first luxury houseboat was launched in 2022 in Chilika, and work is underway to introduce cruise vessels in Hirakud and Chilika. Incidentally, the Tampara Lakefront Development Project won the award for the Best Cafeteria 2023 in the country by the Ministry of Tourism, Government of India (GoI), under the Swadesh Darshan Scheme. Culinary tourism was introduced through the launch of Nimantran, a chain of authentic Odia cuisine fine-dining restaurants in Bhubaneswar and Puri.

The state government has been promoting destination-based tourism because Odisha holds vast potential in thematic tourism, such as beach tourism, heritage tourism and nature tourism. The Patnaik government took up the holistic development of over a dozen destinations. In addition, development based on an infrastructure gap assessment has been initiated for 33 identified tourist destinations in the state.

In 2016, the Baristha Nagarika Tirtha Yatra Yojana was launched by the Chief Minister. Under this scheme, pilgrimage tours to various parts of the country have been provided to more than 19,000 senior citizens from below-poverty-line families. According to an agreement signed between Odisha Tourism and the Indian Railway Catering and Tourism Corporation, nearly 20 pilgrimage tours have been organized.

The state government has undertaken several steps to develop tourism projects across Odisha to meet the United Nations's Sustainable Development Goals in a timely manner. The momentum for this was provided by Odisha Tourism Policy 2022, which superseded the 2016 policy. The state government has envisaged accelerated growth in the tourism sector through professional management and private sector participation, promising lucrative returns on investment for investing stakeholders.

The Social Sector

The state cannot develop holistically with only good GDP growth, increased FDIs or robust agricultural production.

The social sector must also be adequately taken care of so that the lives of a targeted section of the population—the needy and marginalized—are uplifted. Odisha's government has taken several steps in this direction. At one time, the state was globally infamous for hunger-related deaths. One still recalls the reports of several hunger-related deaths in the Kalahandi–Bolangir–Koraput belt. These are now matters of the past. A paper published by a PhD scholar, Umesh Chandra Sahoo, highlights the steps taken by the state government and the challenges faced.

Biju Krusaka Kalian Yojana (BKKY): The scheme was implemented in 2013–14 to offer free health and accident insurance cover of up to one lakh rupees to five members of every farmer family, including the farmer, to safeguard against health hazards. The BKKY was launched in November 2013 to enrol all farmers' families in the state. Since 2016–2017, more than 58 lakh farmer families have been enrolled. Over 3.5 lakh beneficiaries have been treated, and claims worth ₹18,042.99 lakh have been settled. In 2017–2018, it was programmed to support all farmer families in the state with free health insurance, for which ₹8,811.00 lakh was provisioned.

Niramaya: The free drug distribution scheme was initiated in May 2015. It covered all 32 district headquarters, 4 tertiary hospitals, 27 sub-divisional hospitals and 377 community health centres, with a total of 489 typologies of drugs.

The state has also focused on enhancing human development in the field of health. In particular, the government reduced IMR from 91 in 2001 to 40 in 2014, which is below the national average of 41. Odisha was the first Indian state in 2014–2015 to rapidly work towards and achieve tribal immunization programmes, higher institutional delivery and a reduction in IMR. According to the state's economic survey 2020–2021, the maternal mortality rate fell from 303 in 2004–2006 to 150 in 2016–2017. The recovery and reduced mortality rates (as of 14 November 2020) have been especially heartwarming. At 96.43 per cent, it is better than the all-India rate of 93.07 per cent and the global rate of 66.44 per cent. A similar process has been observed in the state's under-5 mortality rates. In 2010, it was 78, and in 2018, it stood at 44.

Biju Pucca Ghar Yojana (BPGY): It is a scheme for rural housing launched in 2014 to convert all *kucha* homes into *pucca* homes by the end of 2019 for the rural poor. Under the scheme, the beneficiaries would construct their homes with ₹1.30 lakh from the state budget. Under the scheme, the government had, till March 2017, constructed 10 lakh *pucca* houses in rural areas; 22 lakh houses have been constructed in rural areas in the last 10 years through several schemes.

Soon after Patnaik took charge, the government initiated Mission Shakti to amalgamate all women self-help groups (WSHGs) to supply identical guidelines, personnel training and training materials to economically empower such groups. WSHGs continued to be informal groups of 10–20 women members working collectively. The number of WSHGs reached six lakhs in November 2016. Now from 2024 there is a new scheme, Subhadra Yojana, which empowers the woman with yearly financial support.

To strengthen women's participation in politics, the government of Odisha decided to increase reservation for women from 33 per cent to 50 per cent in *panchayats* and municipal bodies under the Orissa Panchayat Laws (Amendment) Bill, 2011. It came into effect from the panchayat elections of 2012.

An Overview

As per the economic survey, Odisha's economy has grown at 7.1 per cent per annum from 2012–2013 to 2019–2020, and the expected growth rate was –4.92 per cent in 2020–2021. The decline in the growth rate for 2020–2021 can be attributed to the devastating impact of COVID-19 on the state's economy. But for the resilience of the state economy and effective management of the pandemic, the decline would have been much sharper.

A comparative analysis of Odisha's growth performance vis-a-vis other Indian states from 2012–13 to 2019–2020 reveals a positive differential trend in the state's average annual growth rate. It indicates that between 2012–2013 and 2019–2020, Odisha's economy grew at an average annual rate of 7.1 per cent, faster than the national average of 6.6 per cent.

Per capita income (PCI): Odisha's PCI rose from ₹48,499 in 2011–2012 to ₹1,04,566 in 2019–2020, an increase of about 115.60 per cent. Odisha's PCI in 2019, at current prices, was higher than that of Bihar, Uttar Pradesh, Jharkhand, Meghalaya, Madhya Pradesh and Chhattisgarh.

Poverty reduction: From 2004–2005 to 2011–2012, the state achieved higher poverty reduction at 24.6 percentage points than the national reduction at 15.3 percentage points. This was possible due to a stable government and its effective interventions.

Exports: The value of goods exported from Odisha exhibits an increasing trend from 2011–2012 to 2017–2018. Barring patchy declines, exports from the state moved up from 2011–2012 to 2019–2020.

Tackling rural poverty: Rural poverty in Odisha has reduced by 25 percentage points between 2004–2005 and 2011–2012 (from 60.8 per cent to 35.69 per cent), which is higher than the national reduction by 16 percentage points. Similarly, the poverty gap ratio fell by 10.36 per cent for rural Odisha compared with 4.59 per cent for rural India.

A total of 3,94,212 houses were completed under government schemes in 2019–2020, of which 3,57,914 were under the Pradhan Mantri Awas Yojana (Grameen), 15,567 were under the Biju Pucca Ghar Yojana, 1,858 under the Pucca Ghar Yojana (Mining), 10,983 under the Nirman Shramik Pucca Ghar Yojana and 7,890 under BPGY (Titli).

The Mahatma Gandhi National Rural Employment Guarantee Scheme provided employment of 1,115.72 lakh person days during 2019–2020, an increase from 830.3 lakh in 2018–2019, covering 23.27 lakh rural households in 2018–2019 and 31.86 lakh in 2019–2020. The annual growth rate of providing employment to households in 2019–2020 was 36.9 per cent. The state government has been able to complete the construction of 25,70,174 houses by the end of the financial year 2019–2020 for the most deserving rural poor households.

Infrastructure Development

The Odisha government has taken various initiatives for infrastructure development in the state. These initiatives were led by the Infrastructure Development Corporation of Odisha (IDCO).

Special Economic Zones (SEZs): IDCO has set up two SEZs. The Infocity SEZ has been developed in Chandaka (Bhubaneswar) over an area of 145.91 acres. Reputed organizations, such as Mind Tree, TCS and WIPRO, have established units in this SEZ. Work on a sector-specific IT/ITES SEZ is under implementation at Gaudakasipur near Bhubaneswar (Info

Valley) over an area of 262 acres. Infosys is the anchor tenant for this SEZ; it has been allotted 50.909 acres of land in the park.

Electronic Manufacturing Cluster (EMC): IDCO has been developing an electronic hardware manufacturing cluster at Info Valley under the EMC scheme of the Ministry of Electronics and Information Technology, GoI. The EMC would be established over an area of 203.37 acres at a project cost of ₹2,00,75,18,881 with funding from the GoI and the state government. The land has been demarcated, and development works such as the internal road, boundary wall, land, R&D centre, common facility building, flatted factory building, worker's hostel and administrative building are in progress at the time of writing.

Petroleum, Chemical and Petrochemical Investment Region (PCPIR): Under the PCPIR scheme of the GoI, the Odisha government is developing a PCPIR in Paradip, which will be built on 70,214 acres of land across the Jagatsinghpur and Kendrapada districts. The PCPIR hub is expected to attract investments worth ₹2.74 lakh crore. Indian Oil Corporation Ltd. (IOCL) is the anchor tenant for the project. Around 3,300 acres of land have been acquired and handed over to IOCL for its 15 million tonnes per annum (mtpa) oil refinery, with an investment of approximately ₹30,000 crore.

IOCL has also announced the development of a 700 KT per annum polypropylene unit in Paradip with an investment of ₹3,150 crore. IDCO has formed a special purpose vehicle (SPV), Paradip Investment Region Development Limited, to develop the required infrastructure for the project. It has acquired approximately 7,400 acres of land for industrial development in the PCPIR.

IOCL has also signed an MoU with Dhamra Port Company Ltd. (DPCL) for a 5 mtpa liquefied natural gas (LNG) terminal within the port premises at a cost of ₹5,000 crore. IOCL entered into an MoU with the Odisha government to develop natural gas infrastructure. The natural gas availability from this terminal is expected to boost downstream industries in the PCPIR region.

Special Investment Region (SIR): Based on the development of Dhamra Port and the upcoming LNG terminal facility by IOCL at Dhamra, the government is contemplating developing an SIR over 10,000 acres of land in 43 villages; it has been notified as a lease-barred area. A special act has also been prepared. The SIR shall have delineated zones for industrial, social, logistics and residential purposes. It shall create opportunities for manufacturing industries in the downstream sectors of aluminium and steel, fertilizer and other gas-based and wood-based industries. IDCO obtained in-principle approval to establish the SIR at Dhamra under the Regional Investment Manufacturing Zone scheme of the Department of Economic Affairs, GoI.

Kalinganagar National Investment Manufacturing Zone: The steel complex at Kalinganagar has been established over 13,000 acres, where nine major steel companies, producing 3.5 million tonnes of steel per annum, have already set up their units. It has generated employment for 40,000 people. The Odisha government is planning to develop this complex as a National Investment Manufacturing Zone (NIMZ) under the National Manufacturing Policy of the GoI. Final approval has already been obtained from the Department of Industrial Policy and Promotion (DIPP), GoI, to establish the NIMZ at Kalinganagar. IDCO is the nodal agency for the implementation of the scheme.

Plastic Park in Paradip: To promote industries in the plastic and polymer sector, a plastic park is being developed in PCPIR at IOCL's Refinery Complex under the Plastic Park Scheme of the Department of Chemicals and Petrochemicals, GoI, with an investment of ₹106 crore. IDCO has taken up work on the project.

Seafood Park, Deras: IDCO is developing a Seafood Park in Deras over an area of 152.78 acres. The project is being developed under the Mega Food Parks Scheme of the Ministry of Food Processing Industries (MoFPI), GoI.

Aluminium Park: To promote investment in downstream and ancillary units in the aluminium sector, the Angul Aluminium Park is being jointly developed by IDCO and National Aluminium Company Limited (NALCO) over 223 acres in Angul in the first phase. The project will be developed under the Modified Industrial Infrastructure Up-Gradation Scheme (MIIUS) of DIPP, Ministry of Commerce & Industry, GoI. It received final approval in August 2015. The approved project cost is ₹99.60 crores, including a central grant of ₹33.44 crores.

Convention-cum-Trade Zone Centre: IDCO is also engaged in the development of a convention centre at Janata Maidan in Bhubaneswar. It will include an auditorium with a seating capacity of 4,000.

Tower-2010 in Mancheswar: To provide built-up space to promote IT/ITES industries in the state, IDCO has taken up the construction of a G+17 storey building with a 4.52 lakh square feet super-built-up area. The building is structurally complete.

IT Incubation Centre: An IT incubation centre is being developed at Infocity IT/ITES SEZ, Chandaka, Bhubaneswar, over 2.39 acres with a built-up area of 33,048 m². This complex will have two towers with a 200-seat IT incubator, built-up space for IT/ITES companies, a commercial complex and other amenities. Export-oriented software companies can take advantage of such facilities to start their operations before moving to their regular development centre. Small-scale industries' (SSI) IT/ITES units that have export orders can move to this location for immediate operation.

Development of National Waterways: To develop an inland navigation system for the movement of cargo from industries and mines to ports, an MoU has been signed among the Government of Odisha, Inland Waterways Authority of India, Paradip Port Trust and Dhamra Port for the stretch between Talcher to Paradip and Dhamra of National Waterway-5. IDCO, on behalf of the state government, shall spearhead the SPV to develop permanent terminal facilities for bulk cargo handling at Jokadia/Pankpal and other locations. Meanwhile, an SPV, Inland Water Ways Consortium Odisha Limited, has been formed. IDCO, PPT and DPCL are its members.

Textile Park at Dhamnagar: IDCO also decided to establish a Textile Park and a Food Park over 234 acres near Dhamnagar in the Bhadrak district. The Textile Park shall be developed over 110 acres. An area of 58.625 acres has been allotted to IOCL to set up the manufacturing unit of the Textile Park.

Skill Development

The Odisha government has, over the years, taken several measures to enhance skill development among the state's youth, something NITKAL is also engaged in achieving. The Department of Skill Development and Technical Education plays an important role and has tied up with several training partners to impart skills in sectors such as healthcare, hospitality and IT.

Good Governance is the Key to Development

As the economic survey of 2020–2021 notes, 'Good governance is associated with efficient and effective administration in a democratic framework, which is citizen-friendly, citizen caring and responsive administration. In general, good governance is perceived as a normative principle of administrative law, which obliges the State to perform its functions in a manner that promotes the values of efficiency, non-corruptibility and responsiveness to civil society.'[33]

Some methods adopted are as follows: (1) participatory budget initiative by the finance department; (2) the delivery of public services through the Odisha Right to Public Services Act, 2012; (3) Right to Information (4) law and order through the Crime and Criminal Tracking Network and Systems and Emergency Response Support System; (5) tackling corruption by registering cases; (6) maintaining transparency through E-abhijoga; (7) major e-governance and Information and Communications Technology (ICT) interventions by different departments;

The Way Forward

I believe there is much more to do to make Odisha a leading driver of industrial and agricultural growth in the country. Financial allocation in the health sector via public and private investment must be substantially increased.

---

[33]'Economic Survey 2020-21', *Government of India*, January 2021, https://tinyurl.com/447dbkcw. Accessed on 23 February 2025.

Agriculture and allied sectors remain the mainstay of the state's economy because more than 60 per cent of the population depends on them for their livelihood. Irrigation facilities, crop diversification, integrated farming and the development of animal husbandry and fisheries must be boosted. Natural disaster mitigation measures and mechanisms must be strengthened to minimize the adverse impacts of recurring natural crises, given the geographical location of the state. Special attention needs to be given to the ecotourism sector.

With the many schemes and programmes the state government has unveiled, Odisha is on the road to rapid growth and development in all spheres of activity. In my personal capacity as part of NITKAL, I see an exciting future for us to contribute to the well-being and prosperity of Odisha.

17
Meeting Inspirational Leaders

As a corporate executive and later an independent entrepreneur based in Japan, I have had the privilege of meeting and interacting with many prominent public figures from India. Each of them has unique qualities and strengths, but some common traits among them are their unwavering commitment to India's betterment, their connection with the masses and their rise from the grassroots. Their success inspired me, and I related to several of them because I, too, came from a humble background and achieved some success through hard work, commitment and a belief in my abilities. Like them, I did not let obstacles hinder my determination to achieve what I had set out to.

Droupadi Murmu

Millions of Indians were excited when Droupadi Murmu became the president of India in 2022. She was from a scheduled tribe and had faced and overcome many struggles and challenges in life. Murmu is, in many ways, an idol, an example of what a human being can achieve if only they have self-confidence and show mettle against all odds.

Her appointment as India's head of state was an especially joyful occasion for my family and me. After all, she hails from the Mayurbhanj region of Odisha and comes from the same town as my wife.

I first met Murmu in October 2022 at the imposing Rashtrapati Bhawan in New Delhi. I was visiting Odisha for the Durga Puja celebrations when I received an invitation from the Rashtrapati Bhawan. The President was meeting a select group of people from Odisha, and an acquaintance had suggested my name. I don't have to tell you how excited I was to get this opportunity to meet her. I went there on the scheduled date with my wife. She greeted us warmly, and I was instantly struck by her humble persona. We spoke in Odia, in the Mayurbhanj dialect, which delighted her. On learning that my wife was from her town, Murmu was doubly pleased and asked which ward my wife came from.

She spoke passionately about her home state and wanted to know what I was doing for the betterment of the state's people. I explained to her the many initiatives NITKAL had undertaken in agriculture, skill development, digital and IT, and healthcare, with a focus on the opportunities Japan held for the youth of Odisha. President Murmu listened carefully, but her attention was more on the prospects in the agricultural sector. She asked many questions in that regard. She expressed happiness that I, a native of Odisha, had made it big in Japan.

She was pleasantly surprised when I informed her of the annual Jagannath Rath Yatra the Odia diaspora organized in Japan, in addition to several programmes that showcased Odisha's cultural legacy. On learning that it was my first visit to the Rashtrapati Bhawan, she directed one of her officials to show my wife and me around the premises.

I requested her to visit Japan, on which occasion a large-scale cultural event would be held. She was receptive to the idea. I have remained in touch with her office since then and hope that my dream of hosting her in Japan will materialize.

Narendra Modi

I met Prime Minister Narendra Modi in Japan more than five times over the last nine years. The first was when he visited Japan in August 2014 for the first time as India's prime minister. Modi was already known in Japan, and his friendship with former Prime Minister Shinzo Abe was the talk of the town. The two first met when Modi was the chief minister of Gujarat and was on a trip to Japan to attract investments. The two leaders struck an instant rapport, and their friendship was further cemented after Modi became prime minister.

In a touching tribute for *The Japan Times* after Abe was tragically assassinated in July 2022, Modi said, 'I have lost a dear friend. I first met him in 2007, during my visit to Japan as the Chief Minister of Gujarat. Right from that first meeting, our friendship went beyond the trappings of office and the shackles of official protocol. [...] And, I will always cherish the singular honour of having been invited to his family home in Yamanashi prefecture, nestled among the foothills of Mt. Fuji. Even when he was not the Prime Minister of Japan between 2007 and 2012, and more recently after 2020, our personal bond remained as strong as ever.'[34]

Prime Minister Modi's first visit was grand, which attracted a lot of headlines in Japan and India. Besides

---

[34] '"My Friend, Abe San": PM Modi Pens Emotional Note for Late Japanese PM', *India Today*, 9 July 2022, https://tinyurl.com/yfrjnptc. Accessed on 23 February 2025.

his official engagements, the highlight was his interaction with the Indian diaspora. This practice of meeting Indian community members began with Vajpayee when he came to Japan on an official visit. The Indian diaspora then was negligible. Later, Manmohan Singh visited Japan as prime minister, but that visit did not cause any ripples because he stuck to the official engagement and returned. Modi came months after securing a big victory in the general elections back home and was riding the popularity wave. Naturally, his visit was greatly anticipated in Japan.

My first meeting with Modi was at an Indian diaspora event and later at a business event. I was with L&T at that time, which gave me some weightage. A business delegation had also arrived, which included L&T Chairman A.M. Naik, Azim Premji, Sushil Ruia, Gautam Adani and others. I was impressed by Modi's personality and his keen understanding of issues. He is a fantastic listener and can surprise people with insightful questions. I was also impressed by his commitment to India's development, and he hammered home that point in every interaction with us. He told us, 'Each of you should bring at least five corporate leaders to India so that they see first-hand the opportunities our country has to offer.' Similarly, to promote tourism, he told members of the Indian community that they should each persuade at least five of their Japanese friends and acquaintances to come to India and savour its diversity and rich cultural and civilizational legacy. 'You are all India's ambassadors in Japan,' he reminded us.

Naveen Patnaik

I first met Naveen Patnaik during his visit to Tokyo in April 2023. I knew of his rise in state politics from a reluctant politician to a consummate administrator who had led his party to victory in elections since he assumed the chief minister's post in 2000.

Patnaik is soft-spoken; he speaks little and to the point. He is also a good listener. When I told him I was from Mayurbhanj, he was even more interested. We spoke in English, and he had many questions. I discussed with him the initiatives our organization had taken for the youth of Odisha in skill development, digital development, agriculture, etc. He was very encouraging and assured me his government would extend all the necessary help.

We had arranged a meeting of the Odia diaspora with him. We shared the stage and addressed the gathering, welcoming him to Japan. I also coordinated his and his team's visits, especially the one-on-one engagements and dinners.

I was already a director of the ICIJ and informed him of the organization's efforts to boost Japan–Odisha collaboration in multiple areas. He expressed happiness that I hailed from Odisha and was keen on doing something for my home state.

Dharmendra Pradhan

I met Union Minister Dharmendra Pradhan, who hails from Odisha, in 2017 and July 2022. In the first instance, he had come to Japan as the minister of petroleum and natural gas. Besides participating in his official engagements, he addressed a community of Odia people. We did not discuss anything specific about Odisha. I was with L&T, and the discussions were mostly about India–Japan issues. However, he appreciated that as a native of Odisha, I had done well in Japan as a business executive.

I met Pradhan again at his office in Shastri Bhavan, New Delhi, five years later; this time, he was the minister of education. We spoke at length about Odisha's development and the contributions our organization and I could make in that respect. He observed that the state would benefit greatly if I continued fostering Odisha–Japan trade and providing opportunities to the youth of Odisha in Japan through skill development in the agriculture, healthcare and digital/IT sectors.

I have met several other prominent personalities from India during my career in Japan, all of which I cherish and from which I have learned a lot.

Mohan Charan Majhi

I first met Mohan Charan Majhi in Odisha in July 2024 after he took over as the chief minister of the state. We met again in August with a Japanese delegation for multiple collaboration and job creation opportunities.

Mohan Majhi lives not far from my native place in Odisha. We have the same culture and have faced similar struggles in life. He is very down to earth, and I reiterated my dedication to creating job opportunities for the Japanese market. I discussed with him the initiatives our organization had undertaken for the youth of Odisha in skill development, digital development, wellness, etc. He was very encouraging and assured me his government would extend all the necessary help.

Others

I had the privilege of interacting with various other officials and eminent personalities, from whom I learned a lot. Among them was the Reserve Bank of India's governor, Shaktikanta Das (I met him in November 2024), who turned out to be down-to-earth and extremely knowledgeable about various topics beyond monetary issues. I also met the late Sushma Swaraj, who was then India's external affairs minister. She left me impressed with her grace and understanding of global issues. I also met former Japanese Prime Minister Yoshihide Suga. An experienced administrator, Suga served as prime minister from 2020 to 2021. Earlier, he had been the chief cabinet secretary during the second term of Prime Minister Shinzo Abe from 2012 to 2020. I was struck by his perceptive insights into domestic and foreign affairs.

I believe inspirational stories of people who attained success against formidable odds strengthen one's resolve. 'If they can do it, why can't I?' is a strong motivator. Looking back on my journey, I recall the many challenges I faced. I recall how I, as a small-town boy, felt lost after venturing into big cities for higher education. I remember the moments of self-doubt, but these were always brushed aside before they hampered my advancement. I had not planned to move to Japan, let alone build a successful career there. I took things as they came, always upgrading my skills along the way. That is the *mantra* for all youngsters wanting to make it big in any field. Remain focused; never lose trust in your abilities; keep working hard, and continue skilling and re-skilling yourselves.

There is no shortcut to success. As former President A.P.J. Abdul Kalam said, 'If you want to shine like a sun, first burn like a sun.'

Acknowledgements

Once I decided to write the book, I shared my resolve with my wife, Jaysree, and our daughter, Debangi. Both were very encouraging, though they wondered how I would find the time to take up this formidable task. I told them I would spare a few hours consistently on the weekends.

Of course, I realized early on that I had no experience in writing. It meant that I would have to seek help from someone experienced in the craft. I came in touch with literary critic Ashutosh Thakur, who came forward with his support. He introduced me to his brother and well-known columnist, author and literary consultant, Atul K. Thakur. At various stages of the book's creation, their support was invaluable and I duly acknowledge it. I also highly appreciate Atul ji for the personal attention he gave to the book and for his support with the publishing pitch. As a first-time author with no history of literary pursuits, this was a turning point for me.

Through Atul ji, I met Rajesh Singh, a reputed editor and author, who had many years of experience in journalism. With his guidance and editorial feedback, the book slowly but surely took shape. I am grateful for his support and pivotal role in the completion of the manuscript.

Jaysree helped me recall quite a few events from after our marriage, incidents I had either forgotten or did not fully remember. Debangi found time from her busy schedule of studies—not to mention the challenge of a different time zone as she is based in the US—to read some of the chapters and give her opinion, from which I greatly benefitted. I must add here that she writes quite well.

Looking back, there are many other people I must thank besides those I have already mentioned. They have helped me enormously at various stages of my life and have inspired me to do better. It is not possible to name all of them here, but the few I wish to acknowledge are Mohan Charan Majhi, the chief minister of Odisha; Naveen Patnaik, the former chief minister of Odisha; Union Minister Dharmendra Pradhan and former Union Minister Bishweswar Tudu; several ministers and key bureaucrats in the Odisha government, including the chief secretary at the time of writing; Professor D. Acharya, former director of IIT-Kharagpur; Hiroshi Kobayashi, CFO of Showa Glove; and Ryuko Hira, chairman of the Hira Group and the Indian Commerce and Industry Association Japan (ICIJ).

Now that the English version is out, I plan to release the Hindi and Odia editions of the book. Hopefully, this dream will also be realized.